PRENTICE HALL MATHEMATICS

COURSE 1

Study Guide & Practice Workbook

PEARSON
Prentice Hall

Boston, Massachusetts
Upper Saddle River, New Jersey

ISBN: 0-13-125455-3
6 7 8 9 10 07 06

Study Guide & Practice Workbook

Contents

Answers appear in the back of each Grab & Go File.

Contents (cont.)

Reteaching 1-1

Millions Period			Thousands Period			Ones Period		
Hundreds	Tens	Ones	Hundreds	Tens	Ones	Hundreds	Tens	Ones
		4	2	0	1	5	7	8

4 million   201 thousand   578

- *Standard form:* 4,201,578
- To find the value of a digit, multiply the digit by its place value.

  4 stands for 4 × 1,000,000, or 4,000,000
- *Expanded form:*
  4,201,578 = 4,000,000 + 200,000 + 1,000 + 500 + 70 + 8

Write each number in standard form.

1. six thousand one hundred four

   _____

2. fifteen million twenty-one thousand

   _____

3. sixty thousand one hundred twelve

   _____

4. 2 billion, 9 million, 6 thousand, 1

   _____

5. seventeen thousandths

   _____

6. twenty-nine hundredths

   _____

7. eight thousand two hundred ninety

   _____

8. one billion thirty thousand fifty

   _____

Use < or > to complete each statement.

9. 523 ☐ 567

10. 1,292 ☐ 1,192

11. 47 ☐ 45

12. 9,120 ☐ 912

13. 53,010 ☐ 53,100

14. 4,293 ☐ 4,239

15. 783 ☐ 738

16. 4,121 ☐ 4,212

17. 35,423 ☐ 34,587

18. 241,796 ☐ 242,976

19. 182 ☐ 1,820

20. 8,751 ☐ 8,715

Write in order from least to greatest.

21. 782, 785, 783, 790

    _____

22. 1,240; 1,420; 1,346; 1,364

    _____

23. 6,214; 6,124; 6,421; 6,241

    _____

24. 92,385; 92,835; 93,582; 93,258

    _____

25. 45,923; 54,923; 45,932; 54,932

    _____

26. 1,111; 1,011; 1,101; 1,110

    _____

Practice 1-1

Understanding Whole Numbers

Write each number in words.

1. 1,760

2. 84,508

3. 75,398,012

_____   _____   _____

_____   _____   _____

Write each number in standard form.

4. three thousand forty

_____

5. eleven billion

_____

6. one hundred ten

_____

7. 400,000 + 20,000 + 8,000 + 400 + 6

_____

8. 921 million, 750 thousand, 33

_____

9. eighty-two thousand sixty

_____

Write in order from least to greatest.

10. 12; 152; 12,512; 12,722

_____

11. 10; 10,113; 113; 10,130

_____

12. 149; 49; 49,149; 14

_____

13. 1,422; 142; 14,222; 247

_____

Write the value of the digit 6 in each number.

14. 46,051

_____

15. 62,071,357

_____

16. 42,916

_____

17. 1,063,251

_____

18. 816,548

_____

19. 70,642,050

_____

Use < or > to make each sentence true.

20. 12,680 ☐ 12,519 ☐ 12,299

21. 25,345 ☐ 25,391 ☐ 25,307

22. 7,657 ☐ 7,650 ☐ 7,655

23. 101,321 ☐ 141,321 ☐ 182,321

Reteaching 1-2

Ones	Tenths	Hundredths	Thousandths
2	3	6	9

2 and 369 thousandths

- *Standard form:* 2.369
- To find the value of a digit, multiply the digit by its place value.

  9 stands for 9×0.001 or 0.009
- *Expanded form:*

  $2.369 = 2 + 0.3 + 0.06 + 0.009$

Write each decimal in expanded form.

1. 3.6

2. 4.72

3. 1.283

4. 21.5

5. 7.03

6. 15.308

7. 32.27

8. 6.475

Write each decimal in words.

9. 0.2

10. 0.15

11. 0.29

12. 0.11

13. 0.60

14. 0.9

15. 0.50

16. 0.4

17. 0.37

Write each decimal in standard form.

18. seven tenths

19. one tenth

20. four hundredths

21. seven hundredths

22. twenty-two hundredths

23. forty-six hundredths

24. eighty hundredths

25. thirty hundredths

26. three hundredths

Practice 1-2

Write each decimal in expanded form.

1. 213.23

2. 5.625

3. 19.01

4. 7,430.25

5. 81.8887

6. 3.70917

Write each decimal in words.

7. 12.873

8. 8.0552

9. 0.00065

Write each decimal in standard form.

10. three tenths

11. fifty-two hundredths

12. eight tenths

13. two hundredths

14. seventy-nine hundredths

15. forty hundredths

16. six and five thousandths

17. nine hundred fifty-four ten thousandths

18. $20 + 0.01 + 0.003 + 0.0008$

19. $30 + 4 + 0.9 + 0.02$

20. forty and eight hundredths

21. $200 + 10 + 0.04$

What is the value of the digit 7 in each number?

22. 0.7

23. 4.00712

24. 2.179

25. 28,467.089

26. 348.92971

27. 72.14

Reteaching 1-3

Comparing and Ordering Decimals

Use >, <, or = to show how 4.092 and 4.089 compare.

① Write the numbers on grid paper with the decimal points lined up.

4	.	0	9	2
4	.	0	8	9

② Compare digits in the greatest place. Move to the right until you find digits that are not the same.

4 ones = 4 ones
0 tenths = 0 tenths
9 hundreths > 8 hundreths

So, 4.092 > 4.089.

To order numbers from least to greatest:

① Write the numbers on grid paper (decimal points lined up) and compare.

② Then arrange the numbers from least to greatest.

4.089, 4.09, 4.092

4	.	0	9	2
4	.	0	8	9
4	.	0	9	

Use <, =, or > to complete each statement.

1. 0.01 ☐ 0.15

2. 0.25 ☐ 0.21

3. 0.30 ☐ 0.26

4. 0.10 ☐ 0.12

5. 0.35 ☐ 0.34

6. 0.1 ☐ 0.4

7. 34.4 ☐ 34.40

8. 0.207 ☐ 0.27

9. 0.08 ☐ 0.40

10. 0.32 ☐ 0.309

11. 6.12 ☐ 6.099

12. 0.990 ☐ 0.99

13. 2.36 ☐ 2.036

14. 0.05 ☐ 0.15

15. 1.19 ☐ 1.91

Use place value to order the decimals from least to greatest.

16. 3.46, 3.64, 3.59

17. 22.97, 21.79, 22.86

18. 43, 43.22, 43.022

_____

_____

_____

19. 10.02, 10.2, 1.02

20. 1.09, 1.9, 1.1

21. 7.54, 75.4, 7.4

_____

_____

_____

Order each set of numbers on a number line.

22. 0.67, 0.7, 0.6

23. 0.03, 0.29, 0.019

24. 8.36, 8.01, 8.1

Practice 1-3

Comparing and Ordering Decimals

Use <, =, or > to complete each statement.

1. 0.62 ☐ 0.618 **2.** 9.8 ☐ 9.80 **3.** 1.006 ☐ 1.02 **4.** 41.3 ☐ 41.03

5. 2.01 ☐ 2.011 **6.** 1.400 ☐ 1.40 **7.** 5.079 ☐ 5.08 **8.** 12.96 ☐ 12.967

9. 15.8 ☐ 15.800 **10.** 7.98 ☐ 7.89 **11.** 8.02 ☐ 8.020 **12.** 5.693 ☐ 5.299

Order each set of decimals on a number line.

13. 0.2, 0.6, 0.5

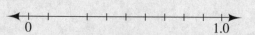

14. 0.26, 0.3, 0.5, 0.59, 0.7

15. Three points are graphed on the number line below. Write statements comparing 0.3 to 0.5 and 0.5 to 0.7.

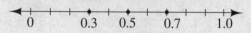

_____

16. Draw a number line. Use 10 tick marks. Label the first tick 0.6 and the tenth tick 0.7. Graph 0.67 and 0.675.

   a. Which is greater, 0.67 or 0.675? _____

   b. How does the number line show which number is greater?

   _____

17. Models for three decimals are shown below.

   a. Write the decimal that each model represents.

   _____

   b. Order the decimals from least to greatest.

   _____

  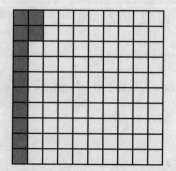

Reteaching 1-4

Estimating with Decimals

To *round* $76.38 to the nearest dollar:

① Find the rounding place. $7<u>6</u>.38

② Look at the digit to the right. $76.<u>3</u>8

③ If that digit is less than 5, leave the digit in the rounding place as is. If the digit is 5 or greater, round up.

$76.38 rounds to $76.

You can use rounding to estimate a sum.

$$3.76 + 0.85 + 4.09$$

Round each number to the ones place.

$$3.76 \longrightarrow 4$$
$$0.85 \longrightarrow 1$$
$$4.09 \longrightarrow \underline{4}$$

Then add.   9

The sum is about 9.

You can estimate decimal products, quotients, sums, and differences by using *compatible numbers*.

Example 1 Estimate the product 9.47×3.81

$$9.47 \longrightarrow 10$$
$$\underline{\times 3.81} \longrightarrow \underline{\times 4}$$
$$40$$

Change to compatible numbers—numbers that are easy to multiply.

The product is about 40.

Example 2 Estimate the quotient $23.96 \div 4.78$.

$$23.96 \div 4.78$$
$$\downarrow \qquad \downarrow$$
$$24 \div 4 = 6$$

Change to compatible numbers—numbers that are easy to divide.

The quotient is about 6.

Round each decimal to the nearest hundredth.

1. 1.679 _____

2. 4.981 _____

3. 12.602 _____

4. 32.9744 _____

5. 0.159 _____

6. 2.008 _____

Round each decimal to the nearest tenth.

7. 6.457 _____

8. 15.0886 _____

9. 0.1235 _____

10. 1.036 _____

11. 25.671 _____

12. 6.390 _____

Estimate each sum or difference.

13. $2.98
   + 7.22

14. $5.33
   + 2.91

15. $10.02
   − 6.89

16. $15.84
   + 37.12

Use compatible numbers to estimate.

17. $7.21 \div 3$

18. $31.74 \div 5$

19. $522 + 81$

20. $908 - 445$

21. $477 + 78$

22. $73 + 229$

Practice 1-4

Estimate by first rounding to the nearest whole number.

1. 0.97×13.21

2. 11.9×4.76

3. 14.7×2.2

_____

_____

_____

4. 18.95×0.76

5. 28.02×1.94

6. 11.93×1.63

_____

_____

_____

7. 43.75×3.17

8. 5.02×3.16

9. 9.04×8.71

_____

_____

_____

Use compatible numbers to estimate.

10. 38.9×19.7

11. $18.47 \div 5.96$

12. $208 + 196$

_____

_____

_____

13. $603 - 204$

14. $76.3 \div 15.1$

15. $93 - 77$

_____

_____

_____

16. $49.1 \div 15.6$

17. $95 + 611$

18. $18.6 \div 2.8$

_____

_____

_____

Use front-end estimation to estimate each sum to the nearest dollar.

19. $\$2.59 + \$3.76 + \$2.41$ _____

20. $\$8.19 + \$2.46 + \$3.57$ _____

21. $\$3.61 + \$2.17 + \$5.84$ _____

22. $\$9.14 + \$8.72 + \$5.63$ _____

Round each decimal to the place of the underlined digit.

23. $1.1\underline{0}9$

24. $2.\underline{3}57$

25. $4.87\underline{7}2$

26. $5.8\underline{0}45$

_____

_____

_____

_____

Tim went shopping and spent $31.79 at each of 3 stores.

27. Use compatible numbers to estimate how much Tim spent altogether.

28. Use rounding to estimate how much Tim spent.

_____

_____

29. Which estimate is closer to the amount Tim actually spent? _____

30. A politician wants to know how many people are in your county or town. Do you think the politician wants to know the exact number of people, or will an estimate be acceptable?

_____

Reteaching 1-5

Adding and Subtracting Decimals

Add 3.25 + 12.6 + 18.93.

First estimate.   3.25   →   3
                  12.6   →   13
                 + 18.93   →   19
                              35

Then follow these steps.

① Line up the decimal points. Write in any needed zeros.

    3.25
   12.6**0**
  + 18.93

② Add as you would add whole numbers. Regroup when needed.

   $\overset{11}{3}$.25
  12.60
  + 18.93
   34 78

③ Place the decimal point.

    3.25
  12.60
  + 18.93
   34.78 ← **Compare to your estimate.**

To subtract decimals, follow similar steps. Work from right to left and regroup when needed. Place the decimal point to complete the subtraction.

First estimate and then find each sum.

1. 0.9 + 6.7

Estimate _____

Sum _____

2. 3.1 + 9.4

Estimate _____

Sum _____

3. 4.88 + 8.19

Estimate _____

Sum _____

Use mental math to find each sum.

4. 14.05 + 9.75

_____

5. 6 + 0.22 + 0.78

_____

6. 9.104 + 5.01 + 7.99

_____

First estimate and then find each difference.

7. 8.5 − 4.2

Estimate _____

Difference _____

8. 7.2 − 3.05

Estimate _____

Difference _____

9. 5.07 − 2.8

Estimate _____

Difference _____

10. 6.347 − 2.986

_____

11. 14.2 − 9.86

_____

12. 13.45 − 5.001

_____

13. 22.7 − 12.06

_____

14. 16.1 − 10.88

_____

15. 1.79 − 0.879

_____

Practice 1-5

First estimate. Then find each sum or difference.

1. 0.6 + 5.8

2. 2.1 + 3.4

3. 3.4 − 0.972

4. 3.1 − 2.076

_____

_____

_____

_____

5. 8.13 − 2.716

6. 5.91 + 2.38

7. 3.086 + 6.152

8. 4.7 − 1.9

_____

_____

_____

_____

9. 9.3 − 3.9

10. 5.2 − 1.86

11. 15.98 + 26.37

12. 9.27 + 15.006

_____

_____

_____

_____

13. 5.9 − 2.803

14. 15.7 − 8.923

15. 4.19 − 2.016

16. 14.75 − 6.9264

_____

_____

_____

_____

17. 5.1 + 4.83 + 9.002

18. 3 + 4.02 + 8.6

19. 4.7 + 5.26 + 8.931

_____

_____

_____

Use mental math to find each sum.

20. 12 + 0.25 + 4.75

21. 18.5 + 0.25 + 0.25

22. 17 + 23 + 10.6

_____

_____

_____

23. 11.3 + 5.7

24. 5 + 6.2 + 4.05

25. 50.6 + 10.4 + 20

_____

_____

_____

26. 2.1 + 0.6 + 0.3

27. 14.3 + 16

28. 4.9 + 0.6 + 4

_____

_____

_____

Use the table at the right for Exercises 29–31.

29. Find the sum of the decimals given in the chart. What is the meaning of this sum?

_____

_____

30. What part of the hourly work force is ages 25–44?

_____

31. Which three age groups combined represent about one-fourth of the hourly work force?

_____

_____

Ages of Workers Earning Hourly Pay

Age of Workers	Part of Work Force
16–19	0.08
20–24	0.15
25–34	0.29
35–44	0.24
45–54	0.14
55–64	0.08
65 & over	0.02

Reteaching 1-6

Lincoln Middle School needs new smoke alarms. The school has $415 to spend. Alarms with escape lights cost $18, and alarms with a false-alarm silencer cost $11. The school wants 4 times as many escape-light alarms as silencer alarms. How many of each kind can the school purchase?

Read and Understand

What facts are needed to solve the problem? *You need the costs of the alarms, $18 and $11; the amount to be spent, $415; and the fact that 4 times as many escape-light alarms as silencer alarms will be bought.*

Plan and Solve

You can try values and check them to solve this problem.
Try: Buy 12 escape-light alarms and 3 silencer alarms.

Check: 12 × $18 = $216
 3 × $11 = $ 33
 Add: $249

$249 is a lot less than the $415 that the school has to spend. Continue with different values until you solve the problem.

Buy 20 escape-light alarms and 5 silencer alarms.

 20 × $18 = $360
 5 × $11 = $ 55
 Add: $415

Look Back and Check

Check to see whether your answer agrees with the information in the problem. *Is the total amount spent $415, or slightly less? Are there 4 times as many escape-light alarms as silencer alarms?*

Choose a strategy to solve each problem.

1. Tina needs batteries. AA batteries cost $3 per pack. D batteries cost $4 per pack. If she has $26 to spend and buys 3 times as many packs of AA batteries as D batteries, how many packs of each does she buy?

2. Ian needs cassette tapes for his recorder. One package of 3 tapes sells for $5. Another pack of 2 costs $4. If Ian has $19 and buys 11 cassettes, how many packs of each kind does he buy?

3. Hyugen has $50 to spend on CDs. New ones cost $9 and used cost $7. He wants to buy more new CDs than used. How many of each can he buy?

4. Frank has $41 to spend on computer disks. A pack of 10 ES brand costs $13 and a pack of 11 CW brand costs $14. How many packs of each can he buy if he spends all his money?

Practice 1-6

Use a problem-solving plan to solve each problem.

1. Philip won a cash prize in a spelling bee. He gave half of his money to his brother. Then he spent $22.50 on a new sweater and put the rest, $56.25, into his savings account. How much money did Philip win?

   _____

2. Gabe, Raul, and Josh competed in a swimming race. Gabe finished in 32.01 seconds, Raul finished in 31.84 seconds and Josh finished in 31.92 seconds. Who came in first, second, and third?

   _____

3. You bought three CDs at the same price. Based on rounding, your estimate of the total cost was $30 before tax. If you rounded to the nearest dollar, what is the maximum price for each CD? What is the minimum price?

   _____

Choose a strategy to solve each problem.

4. Sherrill, Jennifer, Sandy, and Richard competed in a long-jump contest. Jennifer won the contest with a distance of 19.25 meters. Sandy jumped 8.65 meters less than Jennifer. Richard jumped 3.9 meters farther than Sandy but 2.75 meters less than Sherrill. How many meters did Sherrill jump?

   _____

5. In January, Jeff bought three rabbits. By February, the rabbit population had doubled. By March, Jeff noticed that the population of the rabbits had doubled again. How many rabbits will Jeff have by May?

   _____

6. Agatha made a five-digit number with 0, 3, 5, 8, and 9. The number is bigger than 39 and smaller than 53. The thousandths digit is 3 times the tenths digit. What number did Agatha make?

   _____

7. A family of four wants to take the least expensive form of transportation on their vacation. Roundtrip train tickets cost $95.50 per person, roundtrip airline tickets cost $195 per person—buy one get one free—and roundtrip bus tickets cost $64.50 per person plus overnight hotel costs totaling $162.50. Which form of transportation is the least expensive?

   _____

Reteaching 1-7

Multiplying Decimals

Multiply 0.3×1.4. This drawing can help you find 0.3×1.4.

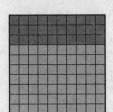 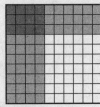

**Each small square is 1 hundredth or 0.01.
Each column or row is 10 hundredths
or 1 tenth or 0.1.**

① Shade 3 rows across to represent 0.3.

② Shade 14 columns down to represent 1.4.

③ The area where the shading overlaps is 42 hundredths or 0.42.

$0.3 \times 1.4 = 0.42$

Compare the result from the model to the result of multiplying the factors.

$$
\begin{array}{r}
0.3 \leftarrow \text{1 decimal place} \\
\times 1.4 \leftarrow +\text{1 decimal place} \\
\hline
12 \\
+ 030 \\
\hline
0.42 \leftarrow \text{2 decimal places}
\end{array}
$$

When multiplying decimals, first multiply the factors as though they are whole numbers. Then add the number of decimal places in each factor to find the number of decimal places in the product.

Write a multiplication statement to describe each model.

1.

2.

_____   _____

For each product place the decimal point in the correct place.

3. $\begin{array}{r} 0.9 \\ \times 2.8 \\ \hline 252 \end{array}$

4. $\begin{array}{r} 3.1 \\ \times 77 \\ \hline 2387 \end{array}$

5. $\begin{array}{r} 6.22 \\ \times 8 \\ \hline 4976 \end{array}$

6. $\begin{array}{r} 19.6 \\ \times 2.03 \\ \hline 39788 \end{array}$

_____   _____   _____   _____

Find each product.

7. $\begin{array}{r} 1.6 \\ \times 3.7 \end{array}$

8. $\begin{array}{r} 8.12 \\ \times 59 \end{array}$

9. $\begin{array}{r} 12.3 \\ \times 6.1 \end{array}$

10. $\begin{array}{r} 5.9 \\ \times 1.2 \end{array}$

_____   _____   _____   _____

11. $\begin{array}{r} 23.4 \\ \times 5.2 \end{array}$

12. $\begin{array}{r} 4.8 \\ \times 42 \end{array}$

13. $\begin{array}{r} 9.2 \\ \times 12.4 \end{array}$

14. $\begin{array}{r} 120 \\ \times 7.6 \end{array}$

15. $\begin{array}{r} 3.15 \\ \times 2.3 \end{array}$

Practice 1-7

Place the decimal point in each product.

1. $4.3 \times 2.9 = 1247$

2. $0.279 \times 53 = 14787$

3. $4.09 \times 3.96 = 161964$

4. $5.90 \times 6.3 = 3717$

5. $0.74 \times 83 = 6142$

6. $2.06 \times 15.9 = 32754$

Find each product.

7. 43.59×0.1

8. 246×0.01

9. 726×0.1

10.
$$\begin{array}{r} 5.342 \\ \times \quad 13 \\ \hline \end{array}$$

11.
$$\begin{array}{r} 0.19 \\ \times \ 0.05 \\ \hline \end{array}$$

12.
$$\begin{array}{r} 6.4 \\ \times \ 0.09 \\ \hline \end{array}$$

13.
$$\begin{array}{r} 240 \\ \times \ 0.02 \\ \hline \end{array}$$

14.
$$\begin{array}{r} 43.79 \\ \times \quad 42 \\ \hline \end{array}$$

15.
$$\begin{array}{r} 0.72 \\ \times \ 0.43 \\ \hline \end{array}$$

Write a multiplication statement you could use for each situation.

16. A pen costs \$.59. How much would a dozen pens cost?

17. A mint costs \$.02. How much would a roll of 10 mints cost?

18. A bottle of juice has a deposit of \$.10 on the bottle. How much deposit money would there be on 8 bottles?

19. An orange costs \$.09. How much would 2 dozen oranges cost?

Find each product. Tell whether you would use mental math, paper and pencil, or a calculator.

20. $19(0.35)$

21. 30×0.1

22. 22.62×1.08

Reteaching 1-8

Multiplying and Dividing Decimals by 10, 100, and 1,000

Example 1: Multiply 10×0.65.

There is one zero in 10 so move the decimal point one place to the right.

$10 \times 0.65 = 6.5$

Check your answer using a paper and pencil.

$$
\begin{array}{ll}
0.65 & \leftarrow \quad \text{2 decimal places} \\
\times 10 & \leftarrow \quad \text{0 decimal places} \\
\hline
6.50 & \leftarrow \quad \text{2 decimal places}
\end{array}
$$

$6.50 = 6.5$

Example 2: Divide $15.5 \div 100$.

There are two zeros in 100 so move the decimal point two places to the left.

$15.5 \div 100 = 0.155$

Check your answer using a paper and pencil.

$$
\begin{array}{r}
0.155 \\
100\overline{)15.5} \\
-100 \\
\hline
550 \\
-500 \\
\hline
500 \\
-500 \\
\hline
0
\end{array}
$$

Use mental math to find each product.

1. 2.7×10 _____

2. $2.5(10)$ _____

3. $100(0.21)$ _____

4. 0.77×100 _____

5. $10 \times 0.2 \times 1$ _____

6. $5 \times 0.2 \times 100$ _____

7. 2.64×100 _____

8. $7.5 \cdot 1,000$ _____

9. $0.5 \times 2 \times 20$ _____

Use mental math to find each quotient.

10. $0.4 \div 10$ _____

11. $2.3 \div 100$ _____

12. $7 \div 100$ _____

13. $52.3 \div 10$ _____

14. $3 \div 1,000$ _____

15. $41 \div 100$ _____

Use <, =, or > to complete each statement.

16. $2.2 \times 10 \;\square\; 2.2(10)(0.1)$

17. $1.1 \div 10 \;\square\; 110 \div 100$

18. $60 \div 100 \;\square\; 600 \div 10$

19. $5 \times 0.3 \times 2 \;\square\; 10 \times 0.3$

20. $0.22 \div 10 \;\square\; 0.22 \div 0.1$

21. $0.004 \times 100 \;\square\; 10 \times 10 \times 0.004$

22. $5.5 \times 2 \times 10 \;\square\; 5.5 \times 100$

23. $(2 \times 5)\,0.14 \;\square\; 0.14\,(10)$

Practice 1-8

Multiplying and Dividing by 10, 100, and 1,000

Use mental math to find each product.

1. 8.7×100

2. $6.5(1 \cdot 10)$

3. $10(6.21)$

_____

4. 5.97×100

5. $4 \times 0.2 \times 5$

6. $3 \times (0.8 \times 1)$

_____

7. 5.23×100

8. $0.38 \cdot 1,000$

9. $(5)(4.2) \times 10$

_____

10. $1,000(2.7)$

11. $(1 \times 100)4.6$

12. $25 \cdot 7.1 \cdot 4$

_____

Use mental math to find each quotient.

13. $7.8 \div 10$

14. $8.91 \div 100$

15. $10\overline{)46.3}$

_____

16. $0.6 \div 10$

17. $1.45 \div 10$

18. $62.3 \div 100$

_____

19. $100\overline{)0.76}$

20. $608 \div 100$

21. $4.1 \div 10$

_____

22. $128.3 \div 10$

23. $10\overline{)16.2}$

24. $6.83 \div 100$

_____

Use <, =, or > to complete each statement.

25. $2.8 \times 10 \ \boxed{} \ 26 \cdot 100$

26. $56 \div 100 \ \boxed{} \ 5.6 \div 100$

27. $3.1 \times 10 \ \boxed{} \ (0.5 \cdot 0.2)3.1$

28. $\$16.20 \div 10 \ \boxed{} \ \$162.00 \div 100$

29. $6.8 \div 100 \ \boxed{} \ 680 + 10$

30. $38.6 \cdot 10 \ \boxed{} \ 2 \cdot 38.6 \cdot 5$

31. $8.3 \cdot 10 \cdot 1 \ \boxed{} \ 8.3 \times 100$

32. $126 \cdot 1,000 \ \boxed{} \ 12.6 \cdot 1 \cdot 100$

Solve.

33. There are 32 rows in a spreadsheet and 100 columns. How many cells are in the spreadsheet? (*Hint:* cells = rows × columns)

_____

34. Paper towels are sold in packages of 12 and 8. You purchased 4 of the 12-packs and 6 of the 8-packs. How many rolls of paper towels did you buy?

_____

Reteaching 1-9

Find the quotient $1.52 \div 0.4$.

You can use a model to estimate the quotient.

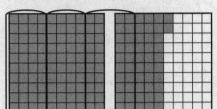

← Draw a model for 1.52.

← Since each square is 0.01, 40 squares represent 0.4.
Circle groups of 0.4.

There are close to four groups of 0.4. The quotient is about 4.

① Multiply the dividend and divisor by 10 so that the divisor is a whole number.

$$0.4\overline{)1.52}$$
$$\quad\curvearrowright\,\curvearrowright$$

② Divide as with whole numbers.

$$\begin{array}{r} 38 \\ 4\overline{)15.2} \\ -12 \\ \hline 32 \\ -32 \\ \hline 0 \end{array}$$

③ Place the decimal point in the quotient above its place in the dividend. Insert zeroes as placeholders if necessary.

$$\begin{array}{r} 3.8 \\ 4\overline{)15.2} \\ -12 \\ \hline 32 \\ -32 \\ \hline 0 \end{array}$$

3.8 is close to 4.

Estimate, then find each quotient.

1. $3\overline{)1.35}$ _____

2. $4\overline{)2.68}$ _____

3. $8.4 \div 6$ _____

4. $8\overline{)27}$ _____

5. $12.96 \div 5$ _____

6. $5\overline{)\$11.30}$ _____

7. $0.4 \div 16$ _____

8. $9\overline{)13.86}$ _____

9. $20\overline{)47.6}$ _____

Use the model to find each quotient.

10.

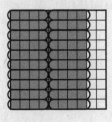

$0.8 \div$ _____ $= 20$

11.

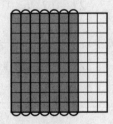

$0.70 \div 0.1 =$ _____

12.

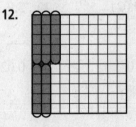

_____ $\div 0.05 =$ _____

Find each quotient.

13. $3 \div 0.12$ _____

14. $1.5\overline{)84}$ _____

15. $78 \div 15.6$ _____

16. $6.4\overline{)23.68}$ _____

17. $7.28 \div 9.1$ _____

18. $3\overline{)4.11}$ _____

19. $0.9\overline{)1.35}$ _____

20. $0.5\overline{)0.935}$ _____

21. $1.9\overline{)19.95}$ _____

Practice 1-9

Dividing Decimals

Draw a model to find each quotient.

1. $0.4 \div 0.08$ _____

2. $0.8 \div 0.4$ _____

3. $0.9 \div 0.15$ _____

Find each quotient.

4. $1.8 \div 6$

5. $16\overline{)3.2}$

6. $17\overline{)5.1}$

7. $9\overline{)21.6}$

_____ _____ _____ _____

8. $15\overline{)123}$

9. $108 \div 5$

10. $50\overline{)17.5}$

11. $24\overline{)120.60}$

_____ _____ _____ _____

12. $9\overline{)11.24}$

13. $14\overline{)889}$

14. $5\overline{)316}$

15. $4.15 \div 5$

_____ _____ _____ _____

Solve.

16. A package of 25 mechanical pencils costs $5.75. How much does each pencil cost?

_____

17. A sales clerk is placing books side by side on a shelf. She has 12 copies of the same book. If the books cover 27.6 in. of the shelf, how thick is each book?

_____

18. The salt content in the Caspian Sea is 0.13 kg for every liter of water. How many kg of salt are in 70 liters?

_____

Find each quotient.

19. $0.4 \div 0.02$

20. $3.9 \div 0.05$

21. $0.2\overline{)26}$

22. $0.4\overline{)1.08}$

_____ _____ _____ _____

23. $0.68 \div 0.2$

24. $0.02\overline{)0.06}$

25. $0.09\overline{)0.108}$

26. $0.04\overline{)0.024}$

_____ _____ _____ _____

Find each quotient. Identify each as a terminating or repeating decimal.

27. $2.5 \div 0.08$

28. $9.6 \div 0.5$

_____ _____

29. $0.25 \div 0.03$

30. $3.2 \div 0.6$

_____ _____

Reteaching 1-10

To find the value of an expression follow the *order of operations.*

First, do all operations inside parentheses.
Next, multiply and divide from left to right.
Then, add and subtract from left to right.

Example 1 Find the value of $6 + (3 + 4) \times 2$.

① Work inside parentheses. $\rightarrow$ **(3 + 4) = 7**
$$6 + \mathbf{7} \times 2$$

② Multiply next. $\rightarrow$ **7 × 2 = 14**
$$6 + \mathbf{14}$$

③ Then, add.
$$6 + 14 = 20$$

Example 2 Compare $10 - (6 \div 2) + 1$ and $(10 - 6) \div 2 + 1$.

First, find the value of each expression.

$10 - (6 \div 2) + 1$		$(10 - 6) \div 2 + 1$
$10 - \quad 3 \quad + 1$		$4 \quad \div 2 + 1$
$7 \qquad + 1$		$2 \qquad + 1$
8		3

Then, use $<$, $=$, or $>$ to compare.
$$8 > 3$$
So,
$$10 - (6 \div 2) + 1 > (10 - 6) \div 2 + 10.$$

Find the value of each expression.

1. $3 + (4 + 1) \times 2$

    a. $4 + 1 = $ _____

    b. _____ $\times 2 = $ _____

    c. $3 + $ _____ $= $ _____

2. $24 \div (5 + 3) - 2$

    a. $5 + 3 = $ _____

    b. $24 \div $ _____ $= $ _____

    c. _____ $- 2 = $ _____

3. $2 + 6 \times 3 \div 3 = $ _____

4. $(6 + 2) \times 3 \div 4 = $ _____

5. $7 + 5 \times 2 - 6 = $ _____

6. $12 \div 3 \times 5 - 6 = $ _____

Use $<$, $=$, or $>$ to complete each statement.

7. $9 + 3 \times 4$ ☐ $9 + (3 \times 4)$

8. $(12 - 4) \times 3$ ☐ $12 - (4 \times 3)$

9. $6 \div 3 + 4 \times 2$ ☐ $(6 \div 3) + 4 \times 2$

10. $3 \times (12 - 5) + 2$ ☐ $3 \times 12 - (5 + 2)$

11. $15 - (12 \div 3)$ ☐ $(15 - 12) + 3$

12. $8 + 2 \times (9 - 7)$ ☐ $8 + (2 \times 9) - 7$

13. $10 + (10 \div 5)$ ☐ $10 + 10 \div 5$

14. $20 - (2 \times 6)$ ☐ $(20 - 2) \times 6$

Practice 1-10

Which operation would you perform first in each expression?

1. $4 + 6 \times 9$

2. $(7 - 5) \times 3$

3. $14 \div 2 \times 3$

4. $18 - 5 + 3$

5. $5 \times 2 + 6$

6. $(9 + 14) - 8 \div 2$

Find the value of each expression.

7. $8 - 3 \times 1 + 5$

8. $(43 - 16) \times 5$

9. $14 \times 6 \div 3$

10. $100 \div (63 - 43)$

11. $9 \times (3 \times 5)$

12. $7 \times (8 + 6)$

13. $15 - (5 + 7)$

14. $(12 - 9) \times (6 + 1)$

15. $(9 - 3) \times 2$

16. $8 - 3 \times 2 + 7$

17. $(9 - 4) \times 6$

18. $(35 - 5) \times 3$

Use <, =, or > to complete each statement.

19. $5 - 3 \times 1 \ \square \ (5 - 3) \times 1$

20. $(4 + 8) \times 3 \ \square \ 4 + 8 \times 3$

21. $3 \times (8 - 2) \ \square \ 3 \times 8 - 2$

22. $(7 + 2) \times 4 \ \square \ 7 + 2 \times 4$

23. $4 + (20 \div 4) \ \square \ (4 + 20) \div 4$

24. $42 - (35 + 4) \ \square \ 42 - 35 + 4$

25. $(9 - 2) \times 3 \ \square \ 9 - 2 \times 3$

26. $55 + 10 - 7 \ \square \ 55 + (10 - 7)$

Insert parentheses to make each statement true.

27. $6 + 7 \times 4 - 2 = 26$

28. $14 - 5 \div 3 = 3$

29. $27 \div 4 + 5 - 1 = 2$

30. $6 \times 7 + 2 - 1 = 53$

31. Haircuts for boys cost \$7. Haircuts for men cost \$10. If 20 boys and 20 men went to the barber yesterday, how much did the barber earn?

Reteaching 2-1

Find the next three numbers in the pattern.

3, 9, 15, 21, ?, ?, ?

Look at how the second number can be found from the first.

3, 9, 15, 21   or   3, 9, 15, 21
× 3   ⟨3 × 3 = 9⟩   + 6   ⟨3 + 6 = 9⟩

Look at how the third number can be found from the second.

3, 9, 15, 21   or   3, 9, 15, 21
× 3   ⟨3 × 3 is not 15.⟩   + 6 + 6   ⟨9 + 6 = 15⟩

Try adding 6 to the third number.

3, 9, 15, 21
+ 6 + 6 + 6   ⟨15 + 6 = 21⟩

Now you can write a rule to describe the pattern. The rule is *Start with the number 3 and add 6 repeatedly.*

3, 9, 15, 21, 27, 33, 39
+ 6 + 6 + 6 + 6 + 6 + 6

The next three numbers in the pattern are 27, 33, and 39.

Find the next three numbers and write a rule for each number pattern.

1. 2, 5, 8, 11, _____, _____, _____

_____

2. 3, 6, 12, 24, _____, _____, _____

_____

3. 9, 18, 27, 36, _____, _____, _____

_____

4. 64, 56, 48, 40, _____, _____, _____

_____

5. 1, 4, 16, 64, _____, _____, _____

_____

6. 75, 70, 65, 60, _____, _____, _____

_____

7. 90, 81, 72, 63, _____, _____, _____

_____

8. 4, 8, 16, 32, _____, _____, _____

_____

Practice 2-1

Sketch the next two designs in each pattern.

1.

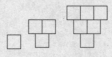

2.

Write the next three terms in each pattern.

3. 3, 5, 7, 9, _____

4. 34, 31, 28, 25, _____

5. 2, 6, 18, 54, _____

6. 12, 20, 28, 36, _____

7. 54, 53, 52, 51, _____

8. 7, 8, 10, 13, _____

Find the next three terms and write a rule to describe each number pattern.

9. 4, 7, 10, 13, _?_, _?_, _?_

_____

_____

_____

10. 2, 4, 8, 16, _?_, _?_, _?_

_____

_____

_____

11. 19, 29, 39, 49, _?_, _?_, _?_

_____

_____

_____

12. 8, 11, 14, 17, _?_, _?_, _?_

_____

_____

_____

13. 135, 125, 115, 105, _?_, _?_, _?_

_____

_____

_____

14. 5, 10, 20, 40, _?_, _?_, _?_

_____

_____

_____

15. Write the first five terms in a number pattern starting with the number 6. Write the rule that describes your pattern.

_____

_____

Find the missing term.

16. 7, 21, 63, _?_, 567

17. 33, 27, _?_, 15, 9

18. 14, 23, 32, _?_, 50

19. _?_, 20, 80, 320, 1,280

_____   _____   _____   _____

Reteaching 2-2

Numerical expressions are made up of numbers and operation symbols.

Algebraic expressions contain one or more variables.
A *variable* is a letter that stands for an unknown number.

You can model algebraic expressions using objects.

The 3 paper clips represent 3 of the same variable.

$3p + 4$

Example 1:
$6 + 3 \qquad 9 \times 2 + 1$

Example 2:
$x + 4 \times 2 \qquad a - b$

You can evaluate the algebraic expression $3p + 4$ if you know a value for p.

① Think of each paper clip as having a value of 6.

$3p + 4$ for $p = \mathbf{6}$ means $3 \times \mathbf{6} + 4$

② Then use the order of operations to evaluate.

$3p + 4 = 3 \times 6 + 4$
$\qquad = 18 + 4$
$\qquad = 22$

Write an algebraic expression for each model.

1.

_____

2.

_____

3.

_____

Evaluate each expression.

4. $3t - 4$ for $t = 8$

$3 \times$ ___ $- 4 =$ ___

5. $7c$ for $c = 6$

$7 \times$ ___ $=$ ___

6. $k \div 2$ for $k = 20$

___ $\div 2 =$ ___

7. $15 + m$ for $m = 6$

_____

8. $2x + 1$ for $x = 3$

_____

9. $5y - 10$ for $y = 6$

_____

10. $4m + 8$ for $m = 5$

_____

11. $3(4h)$ for $h = 2$

_____

12. $9 - 3r$ for $r = 2$

_____

13. $a - b$ for $a = 5$ and $b = 4$

_____

14. $3ab$ for $a = 3$ and $b = 4$

_____

15. $x + 2y$ for $x = 3$ and $y = 2$

_____

Practice 2-2

Write a variable expression for each model. Squares represent ones.
Shaded rectangles represent variables.

1. _____

2. _____

3. _____

Evaluate each expression.

4. $56 \div b$ for $b = 7$

5. $3m$ for $m = 9$

6. $8n$ for $n = 9$

_____ _____ _____

7. $4y + 6$ for $y = 18$

8. $v + 16$ for $v = 9$

9. $2t - 8$ for $t = 21$

_____ _____ _____

10. $2(4e)$ for $e = 5$

11. $12 - 2g$ for $g = 3$

12. $3pq$ for $p = 3$ and $q = 5$

_____ _____ _____

13. $7n - (m + 18)$ for $n = 4$ and $m = 10$

14. $9r + 16$ for $r = 8$

15. $s(58 + t)$ for $s = 2$ and $t = 7$

_____ _____ _____

16. $24 - 4t$ for $t = 4$

17. $3v + 5k$ for $v = 3$ and $k = 6$

18. $5d - (h + 9)$ for $d = 3$ and $h = 5$

_____ _____ _____

Copy and complete each table.

19.

x	$x + 7$
2	9
5	12
8	
11	
	21

20.

x	$5x$
3	
6	
9	
12	
	75

21.

x	$125 - x$
15	
30	
45	
60	
	50

22.

x	$6x + 5$
2	
4	
	41
8	
10	

23. A cellular phone company charges a $49.99 monthly fee for 600 free minutes. Each additional minute costs $.35. This month you used 750 minutes. How much do you owe?

_____

Name _____ Class _____ Date _____

Reteaching 2-3

These terms are used to describe mathematical operations.

Addition	Subtraction	Multiplication	Division
sum more than increased by total added to	difference less than fewer than decreased by	product times multiplied by	quotient of divided by

You can use the terms above to write algebraic expressions for word phrases.

Word Phrase		Algebraic Expression
the sum of m and 17	$\longrightarrow$	$m + 17$
the difference of x and 12	$\longrightarrow$	$x - 12$
3 times w	$\longrightarrow$	$3w$
the quotient of q and 6	$\longrightarrow$	$q \div 6$

Write an expression to describe the relationship of the data in each table.

1.

n	▪
2	10
4	12
6	14

_____

2.

n	▪
1	3
2	6
3	9

_____

3.

n	▪
8	6
10	8
12	10

_____

Write an expression for each word phrase.

4. 6 increased by y

_____

5. the quotient of 8 and e

_____

6. the difference of h and 3

_____

7. 4 times w

_____

8. the difference of s and 8

_____

9. r divided by 2

_____

10. 5 more than n

_____

11. the product of 6 and m

_____

Practice 2-3

Writing Algebraic Expressions

Write two word phrases for each variable expression.

1. $5m$

_____

_____

2. $8 + b$

_____

_____

3. $15q$

_____

_____

4. $c - 10$

_____

_____

5. $18 \div a$

_____

_____

6. $27 - m$

_____

_____

7. $v \div 21$

_____

_____

8. $8r$

_____

_____

9. $t + 17$

_____

_____

10. Write a word phrase that describes the expression $24 - x$.

_____

_____

11. Write a word phrase that describes the expression $36r$?

_____

_____

Write a variable expression for each word phrase.

12. nine less than t

_____

13. eleven more than a number

_____

14. 700 divided by a number

_____

15. two times the number of windows

_____

16. b divided by seven

_____

17. 81 increased by n

_____

18. twelve times the number of muffin pans

_____

19. $15 times the number of hours

_____

20. 8 less than a number

_____

Reteaching 2-4

Problem Solving: Make a Table and Look for a Pattern

Stony Hollow School District has a softball playoff each spring for its 8 schools. Each school plays 1 game against every other school. The winner is the school with the greatest number of victories. How many playoff games are played in all?

Read and Understand What does the problem ask you to find? *You need to find the total number of playoff games.*
How many times will one school play any other school? *1 time*

Plan and Solve How can you simplify the problem? *Draw a diagram for a few schools. Look for a pattern.*

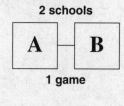

2 schools

1 game

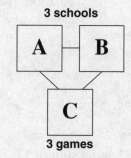

3 schools

3 games

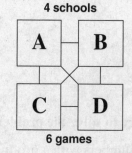

4 schools

6 games

Make a table. Use the pattern you discovered to extend the table to 8 schools.

28 games must be played.

Look Back and Check Does the pattern make sense? *Yes. Each school added to the table plays each of the other schools once. So the number of games added is 1 less than the total number of schools.*

Number of Schools	Number of Games	
2	1	+2
3	3	+3
4	6	+4
5	10	+5
6	15	+6
7	21	+7
8	28	

Solve each problem by making a table and looking for a pattern.

1. School C won the Stony Hollow School District softball tournament. How many games did School C play in all?

   _____

2. If the Stony Hollow School District had 10 schools, how many playoff games would there be in all?

   _____

3. Each umpire is paid $25 per game. There are 2 umpires for each game. What is the total amount paid to umpires for an 8-team playoff?

   _____

4. Suppose one team wins all of its games. Why is it impossible for there to be a tie for the championship?

   _____

Practice 2-4

Problem-Solving Strategy: Make a Table and Look for a Pattern

Solve the problem by making a table and looking for a pattern.

1. A radio station held a contest to give away concert tickets. On the first day, the first caller won. On the second day, the second caller won. On the third day, the fourth caller won. On the fourth day, the seventh caller won. Assuming that this pattern continued, did the thirtieth caller win?

   _____

2. Three drawings are shown. What would the next three look like?

   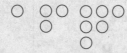

Chose a strategy to solve the problem.

3. Find two numbers with a product of 72 and a sum of 17.

   _____

4. Juana is one year younger than her husband, Leo. The product of their ages is 650. How old is each?

   _____

5. A carpenter charges a basic fee of $25, plus $22 per hour. How much will she charge Ms. Lin if she works for 18 hours?

   _____

6. The product of two numbers is 442. The sum of the two numbers is 43. Find the two numbers.

   _____

7. There are 42 students who signed up for youth camp and 56 students who signed up for family camp. There are 15 students who are signed up for both camps. What is the total number of students who are signed up for camp?

   _____

8. Marquetta charged the Lees a basic fee of $35, plus $25 per hour for repairing their washing machine. What did the Lees pay if it took Marquetta 2.5 hours to finish the job?

   _____

Reteaching 2-5

Using Number Sense to Solve One-Step Equations

One way to solve some equations is to use mental math.

Example 1: Find the solution to the equation.
$a + 5 = 10$

What you think:
If I add 5 to 5, the sum is 10.
$5 + 5 = 10$
So, $a = 5$.

Example 2: Find the solution to the equation.
$y - 9 = 15$

What you think:
If I subtract 9 from 24, the difference is 15,
$24 - 9 = 15$
So, $y = 24$.

Example 3: Find the solution to the equation.
$w \div 5 = 100$

What you think:
$w \div 5$ means w divided by 5.
I know that $500 \div 5 = 100$.
$500 \div 5 = 100$

So, $w = 500$.

Example 4: Find the solution to the equation.
$4w = 24$

What you think:
$4w$ means 4 times w.
I know that $4 \cdot 6 = 24$.

So, $w = 6$.

Use mental math to solve each equation.

1. $4q = 12$

2. $3w = 15$

3. $h + 7 = 16$

4. $h + 2 = 8$

5. $h \div 3 = 12$

6. $m \div 2 = 10$

7. $y - 8 = 12$

8. $w - 5 = 8$

Tell whether each equation is true or false.

9. $100 \div 8 = 25$

10. $18 + 25 = 43$

11. $1{,}100 - 200 = 900$

12. $16 \times 4 = 32$

13. $18 = 9 \div 2$

14. $32 = 16 + 16$

15. $77 + 12 = 99$

16. $2 \times 9 = 81$

Practice 2-5

Using Number Sense to Solve One-Step Equations

Tell whether each equation is true or false.

1. $11 + 7 = 18$

2. $14 = 9 + 6$

3. $8 \times 7 = 42$

_____ _____ _____

4. $3 + 1 + 4 = 7 + 1$

5. $8 \times 13 = 13 \times (6 + 2)$

6. $81 \div 7 = 9$

_____ _____ _____

7. $31 + 4 = 41 + 3$

8. $3 \times (2 + 1) = 2 \times (3 + 1)$

9. $1 \times 6.3 = 1$

_____ _____ _____

Use mental math to solve each equation.

10. $t + 19 = 47$

11. $v + 14 = 76$

12. $94 = y + 32$

13. $86 = a + 29$

_____ _____ _____ _____

14. $w - 53 = 76$

15. $53 = z - 19$

16. $112 = x - 74$

17. $49 = c \div 7$

_____ _____ _____ _____

18. $b \div 24 = 4$

19. $117 = 69 + a$

20. $e - 84 = 79$

21. $62 = g - 27$

_____ _____ _____ _____

Estimate the solution of each equation.

22 $6d = 75$

23. $7m = 24$

24. $10 + x = 43$

_____ _____ _____

25. $a \div 6 = 21$

26. $70 - t = 18$

27. $9b = 42$

_____ _____ _____

28. $60 \div p = 16$

29. $5n = 121$

30. $24 = 49 \div w$

_____ _____ _____

Tell whether the given number is a solution of the equation.

31. $3x + 2x = 10; 2$

32. $9y - 4y = 25; 3$

33. $6 \cdot 3n = 54; 18$

_____ _____ _____

34. The winners of a slam dunk basketball competition receive
t-shirts. The coach pays $50.40 for the entire team, and each
t-shirt costs $4.20. Solve the equation $(4.20)n = 50.40$ to find the
number of team members.

_____

Reteaching 2-6

Addition Equations	**Subtraction Equations**

Addition Equations

There are 4 more than needed to fill the x box.

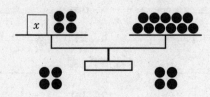

$$x + 4 = 11$$

To *solve* this equation, find the value of x that makes the scales balance.

Since 4 is added to x, subtract 4 from both sides.

$$x + 4 = 11$$
$$x + 4 - 4 = 11 - 4$$
$$x = 7$$

The *solution* to the equation is $x = 7$.

Subtraction Equations

$$r - 3 = 9$$

To *solve* this equation, find the value of r.

Since 3 is subtracted from r, add 3 to both sides.

$$r - 3 = 9$$
$$r - 3 + 3 = 9 + 3$$
$$r = 12$$

The *solution* to the equation is $r = 12$.

Solve each equation.

1. $a + 15 = 31$

$a + 15 - $ ____ $ = 31 - $ ____

$a = $ ____

2. $5 = x - 20$

$5 + $ ____ $ = x - 20 + $ ____

____ $ = x$

3. $19 + t = 51$

_____

4. $p - 11 = 12$

_____

5. $60 = n + 30$

_____

6. $71 = b - 29$

_____

7. $86 + m = 107$

_____

8. $w + 349 = 761$

_____

9. $50 - y = 30$

_____

10. $d - 125 = 75$

_____

11. A car dealer purchased a car for \$2,000 and then sold it for \$3,200. Write and solve an equation to find the profit.

_____

Name _____ Class _____ Date _____

Practice 2-6

Solving Addition and Subtraction Equations

· ·

Solve each equation. Then check each solution.

1. $h + 3.6 = 8.6$

   $h =$ _____

2. $b - 7 = 12.3$

   $b =$ _____

3. $9 + t = 12.4$

   $t =$ _____

4. $10 - a = 3.4$

   $a =$ _____

5. $r + 2.2 = 5.7$

   $r =$ _____

6. $n - 6.2 = 11.4$

   $n =$ _____

7. $8 + j = 15.34$

   $j =$ _____

8. $14.3 - g = 6.3$

   $g =$ _____

9. $m + 7.3 = 9.1$

   $m =$ _____

10. $d - 10.3 = 1.8$

    $d =$ _____

11. $6.3 + f = 10.5$

    $f =$ _____

12. $3.9 - c = 3.1$

    $c =$ _____

13. $q + \$18.30 = \$20$

    $q =$ _____

14. $k - 5.1 = 2.9$

    $k =$ _____

15. $3.89 + x = 5.2$

    $x =$ _____

16. $18.4 - u = 9.6$

    $u =$ _____

17. $e + 2.7 = 10$

    $e =$ _____

18. $r - 7.5 = 3.1$

    $r =$ _____

19. $5.62 + p = 5.99$

    $p =$ _____

20. $8.3 - y = 2.7$

    $y =$ _____

Write and solve an equation. Then check each solution.

21. The top three best-selling albums of all time are Michael Jackson's *Thriller* (24 million copies), Fleetwood Mac's *Rumours* (17 million copies), and Boston's *Boston* (*b* million copies). The three albums sold a combined total of 56 million copies. How many million copies of *Boston* were sold?

    _____

22. Yesterday, Stephanie spent $38.72 on new shoes and $23.19 on computer software. When she was finished, she had $31.18. How much money did she have before she went shopping?

    _____

23. The owner of a used music store bought a compact disc for $4.70 and sold it for $9.45. Write and solve an equation to find the profit.

    _____

Solve each equation.

24. $x - 10 = 89$ _____

25. $n + 14 = 73$ _____

26. $15 - y = 14$ _____

27. $38 + b = 42$ _____

28. $x - 7 = 77$ _____

29. $a + 22 = 120$ _____

30. $42 - z = 16$ _____

31. $19 + m = 19$ _____

32. $d - 6 = 52$ _____

Reteaching 2-7

Solving Multiplication and Division Equations

What value of w makes the scales balance?

$4w = 12$ ⟶ To solve the multiplication sentence, use division.

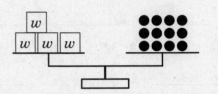

$$4w = 12$$

$$4w \div 4 = 12 \div 4 \longleftarrow \textbf{Divide each side by 4.}$$

$$w = 3$$

The solution is $w = 3$.

To solve a division sentence, use multiplication.

$$y \div 3 = 7$$

$$y \div 3 \times 3 = 7 \times 3 \longleftarrow \textbf{Multiply both sides by 3.}$$

$$y = 21$$

The solution is $y = 21$.

State whether the number given is a solution to the equation.

1. $3g = 36; g = 12$

2. $t \div 8 = 2; t = 4$

3. $h \div 7 = 21; h = 3$

_____

_____

_____

4. $18 = 3m; m = 6$

5. $6a = 18; a = 3$

6. $36 = r \div 9; r = 4$

_____

_____

_____

Solve each equation.

7. $\qquad 12 = 4y$

$12 \div \underline{\quad} = 4y \div \underline{\quad}$

$\underline{\quad} = y$

8. $\qquad n \div 9 = 4$

$n \div 9 \times \underline{\quad} = 4 \times \underline{\quad}$

$n = \underline{\quad}$

9. $23n = 115$

10. $z \div 9 = 9$

11. $48 = 12h$

_____

_____

_____

12. $10w = 150$

13. $34 = t \div 14$

14. $105 = 21t$

_____

_____

_____

15. $64 = e \div 9$

16. $8v = 32$

17. $22 = t \div 4$

_____

_____

_____

18. $3s = 66$

19. $21 = b \div 2$

20. $15n = 45$

_____

_____

_____

Practice 2-7

Solving Multiplication and Division Equations

State whether the number given is a solution to the equation.

1. $8c = 80; c = 10$ 2. $b \div 7 = 8; b = 56$ 3. $9m = 108; m = 12$ 4. $y \div 9 = 17; y = 163$

_____   _____   _____   _____

5. $9r = 72; r = 7$ 6. $14b = 56; b = 4$ 7. $48 = y \div 4; y = 12$ 8. $32 = y \div 8; y = 256$

_____   _____   _____   _____

9. $17a = 41; a = 3$ 10. $w \div 21 = 17; w = 357$ 11. $21c = 189; c = 8$ 12. $52 = y \div 6; y = 302$

_____   _____   _____   _____

Solve each equation. Then check each solution.

13. $905 = 5a$ 14. $6v = 792$ 15. $12 = y \div 12$ 16. $b \div 18 = 21$

_____   _____   _____   _____

17. $80 = 16b$ 18. $19m = 266$ 19. $d \div 1,000 = 10$ 20. $g \div 52 = 18$

_____   _____   _____   _____

21. $672 = 21f$ 22. $z \div 27 = 63$ 23. $43h = 817$ 24. $58 = j \div 71$

_____   _____   _____   _____

Write and solve an equation for each situation.
Then check the solution.

25. Lea drove 420 miles and used 20 gallons of gas. How many miles per gallon did her car get?

_____

26. Ty spent $15 on folders that cost $3 each. How many folders did he buy?

_____

27. Bob pays a $2 toll each way when going to and from work. How much does he pay in four weeks, working five days a week?

_____

28. Julia wants to buy copies of a book to give as presents. How many books can she buy if they are on sale for $12 each, and she has $100 to spend?

_____

Reteaching 2-8

An *exponent* tells how many times a number is used as a factor.

$3 \times 3 \times 3 \times 3$ shows the number 3 is used as a factor 4 times.

$3 \times 3 \times 3 \times 3$ can be written 3^4.

In 3^4, 3 is the *base* and 4 is the exponent.

Read 3^4 as "three to the fourth power."

- To *simplify* a power, first write it as a product.

  $2^5 = 2 \times 2 \times 2 \times 2 \times 2 = 32$

- When you simplify expressions with exponents, do all operations inside parentheses first. Then simplify the powers.

  Example: $30 - (2 + 3)^2 = 30 - 5^2$
  $$= 30 - 25$$
  $$= 5$$

Name the base and the exponent.

1. 3^6

base _____

exponent _____

2. 6^2

base _____

exponent _____

3. 8^4

base _____

exponent _____

Write each expression using an exponent. Name the base and the exponent.

4. $9 \times 9 \times 9$

_____

5. $6 \times 6 \times 6 \times 6$

_____

6. $1 \times 1 \times 1 \times 1 \times 1$

_____

Simplify each expression.

7. 6^2

_____

8. 3^5

_____

9. 10^4

_____

10. $4^2 + 5^2$

_____

11. $2 \times 6 - 2^3$

_____

12. $6^2 + 4^2$

_____

13. $5 + 5^2 - 2$

_____

14. $24 \div 4 + 2^4$

_____

15. $9 + (40 \div 2^3)$

_____

16. $(4^2 + 4) \div 5$

_____

17. $10 \times (30 - 5^2)$

_____

18. $12 + 18 \div 3^2$

_____

Practice 2-8

Write each expression using an exponent. Name the base and the exponent.

1. $3 \times 3 \times 3 \times 3$

_____

_____

2. $7 \times 7 \times 7 \times 7 \times 7 \times 7$

_____

_____

3. $9 \times 9 \times 9$

_____

_____

Write each number in expanded form using powers of 10.

4. 98,364

_____

_____

_____

5. 20,351,401

_____

_____

_____

6. 875,020

_____

_____

_____

Simplify each expression.

7. 9^2

_____

8. 6^4

_____

9. 5^3

_____

10. 7^3

_____

11. $156 + (256 \div 8^2)$

_____

12. $32 + 64 + 2^3$

_____

13. $53 + 64 \div 2^3$

_____

14. $1,280 - 5 \times 6^2$

_____

Find each answer to complete the puzzle.

ACROSS

1. $(3 \times 4)^2$

3. $60 \div (8 + 7) + 11$

4. $2^2 \times 5^2 + 106$

5. $4 + 7 \times 2^3$

6. $7^2 + 4$

9. $48 \div 4 \times 5 - 2 \times 5$

10. $(4 + 3) \times (2 + 1)$

12. $12 \times (30 + 37)$

13. $5 \times (9 + 4) + 362 \div 2$

14. $29 \times 18 \div 9$

DOWN

1. $8 \times (5 + 4) \div 6$

2. $700 \times (2 + 4) \div (17 - 7)$

3. $11 \times (18 - 3)$

5. $60 + (5 \times 4^3) + 2^2 \times 55$

7. $7^2 - 7 \times 2$

8. $(4^2 - 4) \times 10$

9. $2^4 \times 2^5$

11. $(3 + 2) \times (6^2 - 7)$

12. $3^4 + 405 \div 81$

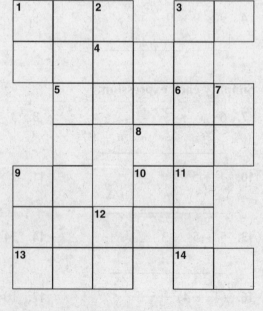

Reteaching 2-9

The *Distributive Property* allows you to break numbers apart to make mental math easier.

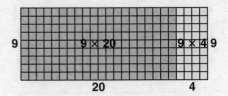

Multiply 9×24 mentally.
Think: $9 \times 24 = 9 \times (20 + 4)$
$= (9 \times 20) + (9 \times 4)$
$= 180 + 36$
$= 216$

The Distributive Property may also help you to simplify an expression.

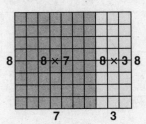

$(8 \times 7) + (8 \times 3) = 8 \times (7 + 3)$
$= 8 \times 10$
$= 80$

Use the Distributive Property to find the missing numbers in the equation.

1. $(\boxed{} \times 4) + (3 \times \boxed{}) = 3 \times (4 + 8)$

2. $(6 \times \boxed{}) - (\boxed{} \times 3) = 6 \times (5 - 3)$

3. $4 \times (\boxed{} - 3) = (\boxed{} \times 9) - (4 \times \boxed{})$

4. $(\boxed{} \times 7) - (6 \times \boxed{}) = 6 \times (7 - 5)$

5. $(4 \times 5) + (\boxed{} \times 7) = 4 \times (\boxed{} + 7)$

6. $\boxed{} \times (12 + 8) = (6 \times \boxed{}) + (\boxed{} \times 8)$

Use the Distributive Property to rewrite and simplify each expression.

7. $(2 \times 7) + (2 \times 5)$

8. $8 \times (60 - 5)$

_____

_____

9. $(7 \times 8) - (7 \times 6)$

10. $(12 \times 3) + (12 \times 4)$

_____

_____

Use the Distributive Property to simplify each expression.

11. 3×27 _____

12. 5×43 _____

13. 8×59 _____

14. 7×61 _____

15. 5×84 _____

16. 6×53 _____

17. 8×48 _____

18. 4×91 _____

19. 9×38 _____

Practice 2-9

The Distributive Property

Write an expression to represent the total area of each figure. Then use your expression to find the total area. Show all your work.

1.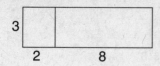

2.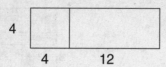

3.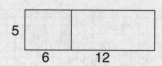

_____   _____   _____

Use the Distributive Property to find the missing numbers in the equations.

4. $8 \times (9 + 4) = (\boxed{} \times 9) + (8 \times \boxed{})$

5. $(4 \times 7) + (4 \times 5) = 4 \times (\boxed{} + 5)$

6. $9 \times (7 - 1) = (9 \times \boxed{}) - (\boxed{} \times 1)$

7. $(5 \times 7) + (5 \times 6) = \boxed{} \times (7 + 6)$

8. $3 \times (7 + 9) = (\boxed{} \times 7) + (3 \times \boxed{})$

9. $8 \times (9 - 6) = (8 \times \boxed{}) - (\boxed{} \times 6)$

Use the Distributive Property to multiply mentally.

10. 7×53

11. 8×97

12. 5×402

_____   _____   _____

13. 8×103

14. 9×213

15. 7×49

_____   _____   _____

Use the Distributive Property to simplify each expression.

16. $9 \times (5 + 3) \times 4 - 6$

17. $(8 + 7) \times 3 \times 2$

18. $5 \times 7 \times 3 + (5 - 4)$

_____   _____   _____

19. $6 \times (8 - 3) + 9 \times 4$

20. $7 \times (8 - 2) \times 4 + 9$

21. $(8 + 6) \times 3 \times 9$

_____   _____   _____

22. The auditorium at the School for the Arts has 102 rows of seats and each row has 7 seats in it. Use the Distributive Property to find the number of seats in the auditorium.

_____

23. The largest television screen ever made was featured at the Tsukuba International Exposition near Tokyo, Japan, in 1985. The screen was called the Sony JUMBOtron and measured 40 meters by 25 meters. Use the Distributive Property to find the area of the screen.

_____

Reteaching 3-1

Divisibility and Mental Math

A number is **divisible** by a second number if the second number divides into the first with no remainder. Here are some rules.

Last Digit of a Number	The Number Is Divisible by	Examples
any	1	any number
0, 2, 4, 6, 8	2	10; 24; 32; 54; 106; 138
0, 5	5	10; 25; 70; 915; 1,250
0	10	10; 20; 90; 500; 4,300

The Sum of the Digits	The Number Is Divisible by	Examples	
is divisible by 3	3	$843 \rightarrow$ $8 + 4 + 3 = 15$ and $15 \div 3 = 5$	281 R0 $3\overline{)843}$
is divisible by 9	9	$2,898 \rightarrow$ $2 + 8 + 9 + 8 = 27$ and $27 \div 9 = 3$	322 R0 $9\overline{)2,898}$

Circle the numbers that are divisible by the number at the left.

1. 2   8   15   26   42   97   105   218

2. 5   14   10   25   18   975   1,005   2,340

3. 10   100   75   23   60   99   250   655

4. 3   51   75   12   82   93   153   274

5. 9   27   32   36   108   126   245   387

Use mental math to determine if the first number is divisible by the second.

6. 185; 5 _____

7. 76,870; 10 _____

8. 461; 1 _____

9. 456; 3 _____

10. 35,994; 2 _____

11. 6,791; 3 _____

12. 12,866; 9 _____

13. 151,002; 9 _____

14. 55,340; 5 _____

15. 6,888; 2 _____

16. 31,067; 5 _____

17. 901,204; 3 _____

18. 2,232; 3 _____

19. 45,812; 9 _____

20. 3,090; 10 _____

21. 312; 9 _____

22. 1,933; 3 _____

23. 28,889; 2 _____

Test each number for being divisible by 2, 5, or 10. Some numbers may be divisible by more than one number.

24. 800 _____

25. 65 _____

26. 1,010 _____

Practice 3-1

Is the first number divisible by the second? Use mental math.

1. 475 by 5 _____   **2.** 5,296 by 3 _____   **3.** 843 by 2 _____   **4.** 76,780 by 10 _____

5. 456,790 by 5 _____   **6.** 3,460 by 2 _____   **7.** 4,197 by 3 _____   **8.** 100,005 by 10 _____

Test each number for divisibility by 2, 3, 5, 9, or 10.

9. 126   **10.** 257   **11.** 430   **12.** 535

_____   _____   _____   _____

13. 745   **14.** 896   **15.** 729   **16.** 945

_____   _____   _____   _____

17. 4,580   **18.** 6,331   **19.** 7,952   **20.** 8,000

_____   _____   _____   _____

21. 19,450   **22.** 21,789   **23.** 43,785   **24.** 28,751

_____   _____   _____   _____

Find the digit that makes each number divisible by 9.

25. 54,78☐   **26.** 42,☐97   **27.** 83,2☐4   **28.** 53☐,904

Name the numbers that are divisible by the numbers given.

29. numbers between 40 and 50, divisible by 3 and 5

_____

30. numbers between 10 and 20, divisible by 2, 3, and 9

_____

31. numbers between 380 and 410, divisible by 2, 5, and 10

_____

32. numbers between 590 and 610, divisible by 2, 3, 5, and 10

_____

33. There are 159 students to be grouped into relay teams. Each
team is to have the same number of students. Can each team
have 3, 5, or 6 students?

_____

Reteaching 3-2

Prime Numbers and Prime Factorization

A *prime number* has exactly two factors, the number itself and 1.

$5 \times 1 = 5$
5 is a prime number.

A *composite number* has more than two factors.

$1 \times 6 = 6$
$2 \times 3 = 6$

1, 2, 3, and 6 are factors of 6.
6 is a composite number.

The number 1 is neither prime nor composite.

Every composite number can be written as a product of prime numbers.

$6 = 2 \times 3$
$8 = 2 \times 2 \times 2$
$12 = 2 \times 2 \times 3$

Factors that are prime numbers are called *prime factors*. You can use a *factor tree* to find prime factors. This one shows the prime factors of 50.

$50 = 2 \times 5 \times 5$ *is the prime factorization* of 50.

Tell whether each number is prime or composite. Explain.

1. 21

2. 43

3. 53

4. 74

_____

5. 54

6. 101

7. 67

8. 138

_____

9. 83

10. 95

11. 41

12. 57

_____

Complete each factor tree.

13.

14.
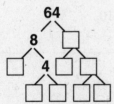

15.
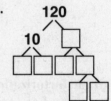

Find the prime factorization of each number.

16. 21

17. 48

18. 81

19. 56

_____

20. 63

21. 100

22. 103

23. 155

_____

Practice 3-2

1. Make a list of all the prime numbers from 50 through 75. _____

Tell whether each number is prime or composite.

2. 53 _____

3. 86 _____

4. 95 _____

5. 17 _____

6. 24 _____

7. 27 _____

8. 31 _____

9. 51 _____

10. 103 _____

11. 47 _____

12. 93 _____

13. 56 _____

Complete each factor tree.

14.

15.

16.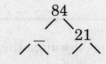

17.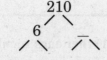

Find the prime factorization of each number.

18. 58 _____

19. 72 _____

20. 40 _____

21. 30 _____

22. 120 _____

23. 100 _____

24. 144 _____

25. 310 _____

Find the number with the given prime factorization.

26. $2 \times 2 \times 5 \times 7 \times 11$ _____

27. $2 \times 3 \times 5 \times 7 \times 11$ _____

28. $2 \times 2 \times 13 \times 17$ _____

29. $7 \times 11 \times 13 \times 17$ _____

30. There are 32 students in a class. How many ways can the class be divided into groups with equal numbers of students? What are they?

_____

Reteaching 3-3

Greatest Common Factor

You can find the *greatest common factor (GCF)* of 12 and 18 using a division ladder, factor trees, or by listing the factors. Two of these methods are shown.

① List the factors of 12 and 18.

12: 1, 2, 3, 4, 6, 12
18: 1, 2, 3, 6, 9, 18

② Find the common factors.

12: ①,②,③, 4,⑥, 12
18: ①,②,③,⑥, 9, 18

The common factors are 1, 2, 3, and 6.

③ Name the greatest common factor: 6.

① Draw factor trees.

② Write each prime factorization. Identify common factors.

12: ②× 2 ×③
18: ②×③× 3

③ Multiply the common factors. $2 \times 3 = 6$. The GCF of 12 and 18 is 6.

List the factors to find the GCF of each set of numbers.

1. 10: _____
15: _____
GCF: _____

2. 14: _____
21: _____
GCF: _____

3. 9: _____
21: _____
GCF: _____

4. 12: _____
13: _____
GCF: _____

5. 15: _____
25: _____
GCF: _____

6. 15: _____
18: _____
GCF: _____

7. 36: _____
48: _____
GCF: _____

8. 24: _____
30: _____
GCF: _____

Find the GCF of each set of numbers.

9. 21, 60 _____

10. 15, 45 _____

11. 32, 40 _____

12. 54, 60 _____

13. 20, 50 _____

14. 21, 63 _____

15. 36, 40 _____

16. 48, 72 _____

17. 90, 150 _____

Practice 3-3

Greatest Common Factor

List the factors to find the GCF of each set of numbers.

1. 8, 12   **2.** 18, 27   **3.** 15, 23   **4.** 17, 34

_____   _____   _____   _____

5. 24, 12   **6.** 18, 24   **7.** 5, 25   **8.** 20, 25

_____   _____   _____   _____

Use a division ladder to find the GCF of each set of numbers.

9. 10, 15   **10.** 25, 75   **11.** 14, 21   **12.** 18, 57

_____   _____   _____   _____

13. 32, 24, 40   **14.** 25, 60, 75   **15.** 12, 35, 15   **16.** 15, 35, 20

_____   _____   _____   _____

Use factor trees to find the GCF of each set of numbers.

17. 28, 24   **18.** 27, 36   **19.** 15, 305   **20.** 24, 45

_____   _____   _____   _____

21. 57, 27   **22.** 24, 48   **23.** 56, 35   **24.** 29, 87

_____   _____   _____   _____

25. 75, 200   **26.** 90, 160   **27.** 72, 108   **28.** 50, 96

_____   _____   _____   _____

Solve.

29. The GCF of two numbers is 850. Neither number is divisible by the other. What is the smallest that these two numbers could be?

_____

30. The GCF of two numbers is 479. One number is even and the other number is odd. Neither number is divisible by the other. What is the smallest that these two numbers could be?

_____

31. The GCF of two numbers is 871. Both numbers are even and neither is divisible by the other. What is the smallest that these two numbers could be?

_____

Reteaching 3-4

Equivalent fractions are fractions that name the same amount.

To find equivalent fractions, multiply or divide the numerator and denominator by the same number.

$$\frac{2}{5} \; = \; \frac{4}{10}$$
$$\times 2$$
$$\times 2$$

$$\frac{4}{10} \; = \; \frac{2}{5}$$
$$\div 2$$
$$\div 2$$

So, $\frac{2}{5} = \frac{4}{10}$.

To write a fraction in *simplest form,* divide the numerator and denominator by their greatest common factor.

Example: Write $\frac{8}{12}$ in simplest form.

① Find the greatest common factor.

8: 1, 2, **4**, 8
12: 1, 2, 3, **4**, 6, 12

The GCF is 4.

② Divide the numerator and denominator by the GCF.

$$\frac{8}{12} \; = \; \frac{2}{3}$$
$$\div 4$$
$$\div 4$$

$\frac{8}{12}$ in simplest form is $\frac{2}{3}$.

Write two fractions equivalent to each fraction.

1. $\frac{5}{6}$ _____

2. $\frac{3}{7}$ _____

3. $\frac{7}{8}$ _____

4. $\frac{3}{11}$ _____

5. $\frac{3}{6}$ _____

6. $\frac{1}{5}$ _____

State whether each fraction is in simplest form. If it is not, write it in simplest form.

7. $\frac{12}{15}$ _____

8. $\frac{8}{15}$ _____

9. $\frac{9}{21}$ _____

10. $\frac{15}{22}$ _____

11. $\frac{14}{30}$ _____

12. $\frac{25}{70}$ _____

Write each fraction in simplest form.

13. $\frac{12}{24}$ _____

14. $\frac{10}{200}$ _____

15. $\frac{56}{64}$ _____

16. $\frac{3}{9}$ _____

17. $\frac{130}{170}$ _____

18. $\frac{12}{16}$ _____

19. $\frac{7}{49}$ _____

20. $\frac{22}{33}$ _____

21. $\frac{30}{225}$ _____

22. There are 420 girls out of 1,980 people attending a state fair. In simplest form, what fraction of the people attending are girls?

_____

Practice 3-4

Name the fractions modeled and determine if they are equivalent.

1.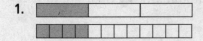

_____

2.

_____

3.

_____

By what number can you multiply the numerator and denominator of the first fraction to get the second fraction?

4. $\frac{2}{3}, \frac{4}{6}$ _____

5. $\frac{3}{8}, \frac{15}{40}$ _____

6. $\frac{7}{10}, \frac{42}{60}$ _____

7. $\frac{3}{4}, \frac{9}{12}$ _____

By what number can you divide the numerator and denominator of the first fraction to get the second fraction?

8. $\frac{6}{8}, \frac{3}{4}$ _____

9. $\frac{70}{80}, \frac{7}{8}$ _____

10. $\frac{15}{60}, \frac{1}{4}$ _____

11. $\frac{75}{100}, \frac{3}{4}$ _____

Write two equivalent fractions for each fraction.

12. $\frac{3}{10}$ _____

13. $\frac{7}{8}$ _____

14. $\frac{5}{6}$ _____

15. $\frac{3}{4}$ _____

16. $\frac{15}{20}$ _____

17. $\frac{8}{12}$ _____

18. $\frac{15}{45}$ _____

19. $\frac{8}{32}$ _____

State whether each fraction is in simplest form. If it is not, write it in simplest form.

20. $\frac{15}{35}$ _____

21. $\frac{22}{55}$ _____

22. $\frac{11}{15}$ _____

23. $\frac{25}{32}$ _____

24. $\frac{34}{36}$ _____

25. $\frac{19}{57}$ _____

26. $\frac{20}{53}$ _____

27. $\frac{125}{200}$ _____

28. $\frac{27}{54}$ _____

29. $\frac{30}{41}$ _____

30. $\frac{9}{17}$ _____

31. $\frac{85}{110}$ _____

32. Use the numbers 2, 5, 8, and 20 to write two pairs of equivalent fractions. _____

33. A library has 10 camping guide books, 4 fishing guide books, and 6 hiking guide books. In simplest form, what fraction of the guide books are camping or hiking guide books?

_____

34. An orchard has 48 apple trees, 30 peach trees, and 42 pear trees. In simplest form, what fraction of the trees are peach trees?

_____

Reteaching 3-5

To write a mixed number as an *improper fraction:*

① Multiply the whole number by the denominator.

② Add this product to the numerator.

③ Write this sum over the denominator.

$$3\frac{5}{8} = \frac{29}{8}$$

To write an improper fraction as a *mixed number:*

① Divide the numerator by the denominator.

$$\frac{20}{8} = 2 \text{ remainder } 4$$

② Write the remainder over the denominator.

$$= 2\frac{4}{8}$$

③ Simplify, if possible.

$$= 2\frac{1}{2}$$

$$\frac{20}{8} = 2\frac{1}{2}$$

Write each mixed number as an improper fraction.

1. $2\frac{2}{7}$ _____

2. $5\frac{3}{4}$ _____

3. $6\frac{1}{2}$ _____

4. $6\frac{5}{8}$ _____

5. $3\frac{4}{10}$ _____

6. $4\frac{3}{5}$ _____

7. $9\frac{1}{3}$ _____

8. $4\frac{4}{5}$ _____

9. $1\frac{7}{8}$ _____

10. $3\frac{3}{8}$ _____

11. $2\frac{3}{7}$ _____

12. $8\frac{1}{6}$ _____

On a separate sheet of paper, draw a model of a 4-inch ruler marked off in eighths. Find and label each measurement on your ruler.

13. $3\frac{5}{8}$

14. $2\frac{6}{8}$

15. $3\frac{1}{2}$

16. $1\frac{3}{4}$

17. $2\frac{1}{2}$

18. $3\frac{1}{4}$

Write each improper fraction as a mixed number in simplest form.

19. $\frac{9}{8}$ _____

20. $\frac{7}{2}$ _____

21. $\frac{12}{5}$ _____

22. $\frac{8}{3}$ _____

23. $\frac{14}{8}$ _____

24. $\frac{6}{5}$ _____

25. $\frac{20}{3}$ _____

26. $\frac{17}{5}$ _____

27. $\frac{18}{4}$ _____

28. $\frac{9}{5}$ _____

29. $\frac{29}{8}$ _____

30. $\frac{24}{9}$ _____

Practice 3-5

Mixed Numbers and Improper Fractions

What mixed number represents the amount shaded?

1.    _____

2.    _____

3.    _____

4.    _____

Write each mixed number as an improper fraction.

5. $1\frac{7}{8}$ _____

6. $2\frac{3}{4}$ _____

7. $7\frac{1}{3}$ _____

8. $8\frac{2}{3}$ _____

9. $3\frac{3}{4}$ _____

10. $4\frac{1}{4}$ _____

11. $5\frac{5}{6}$ _____

12. $1\frac{9}{10}$ _____

13. $2\frac{3}{8}$ _____

14. $4\frac{7}{8}$ _____

15. $2\frac{3}{5}$ _____

16. $6\frac{1}{2}$ _____

17. $3\frac{11}{12}$ _____

18. $2\frac{7}{12}$ _____

19. $5\frac{4}{15}$ _____

20. $2\frac{7}{15}$ _____

Write each improper fraction as a mixed number in simplest form.

21. $\frac{15}{2}$ _____

22. $\frac{8}{3}$ _____

23. $\frac{5}{2}$ _____

24. $\frac{7}{3}$ _____

25. $\frac{11}{10}$ _____

26. $\frac{7}{6}$ _____

27. $\frac{9}{8}$ _____

28. $\frac{20}{8}$ _____

29. $\frac{27}{12}$ _____

30. $\frac{26}{18}$ _____

31. $\frac{35}{21}$ _____

32. $\frac{17}{4}$ _____

33. $\frac{17}{5}$ _____

34. $\frac{17}{6}$ _____

35. $\frac{36}{15}$ _____

36. $\frac{28}{21}$ _____

37. Find the improper fraction with a denominator of 6 that is equivalent to $5\frac{1}{2}$.

_____

38. Find the improper fraction with a denominator of 12 that is equivalent to $10\frac{1}{4}$.

_____

Reteaching 3-6

Least Common Multiple

Find the *least common multiple (LCM)* of 8 and 12.

① Begin listing multiples of each number.

8: 8, 16, 24, 32, 40

12: 12, 24

② Continue the lists until you find the first multiple that is common to both lists. That is the LCM.

The least common multiple of 8 and 12 is 24.

List multiples to find the LCM of each pair of numbers.

1. 4: _____

5: _____

LCM: _____

2. 6: _____

7: _____

LCM: _____

3. 9: _____

15: _____

LCM: _____

4. 10: _____

25: _____

LCM: _____

5. 8: _____

24: _____

LCM: _____

6. 8: _____

12: _____

LCM: _____

7. 4: _____

7: _____

LCM: _____

8. 15: _____

25: _____

LCM: _____

9. 15: _____

20: _____

LCM: _____

10. 4: _____

9: _____

LCM: _____

Use prime factorization to find the LCM of each set of numbers.

11. 9, 21 _____

12. 6, 8 _____

13. 18, 24 _____

14. 40, 50 _____

15. 42, 49 _____

16. 6, 12 _____

Practice 3-6

List multiples to find the LCM of each set of numbers.

1. 5, 10

2. 2, 3

3. 6, 8

4. 4, 6

5. 8, 10

6. 5, 6

7. 12, 15

8. 8, 12

9. 9, 15

10. 6, 15

11. 6, 9

12. 6, 18

13. 3, 5

14. 4, 5

15. 9, 21

16. 7, 28

17. 4, 6, 8

18. 6, 8, 12

19. 4, 9, 12

20. 6, 9, 12

21. 6, 12, 15

22. 8, 12, 15

23. 2, 4, 5

24. 5, 10, 15

Use prime factorization to find the LCM of each set of numbers.

25. 18, 21

26. 15, 21

27. 18, 24

28. 21, 24

29. 15, 30

30. 24, 30

31. 24, 72

32. 18, 72

33. 8, 42

34. 16, 42

35. 8, 56

36. 6, 81

37. 8, 30

38. 16, 30

39. 18, 30

40. 45, 60

41. 12, 24, 16

42. 8, 16, 20

43. 12, 16, 20

44. 15, 20, 25

45. At a store, hot dogs come in packages of eight and hot dog buns come in packages of twelve. What is the least number of packages of each type that you can buy and have no hot dogs or buns left over?

_____

Reteaching 3-7

To compare and order fractions, use the *least common denominator (LCD)*.
The LCD is the least common multiple (LCM) of the original denominators.

Compare Fractions	**Order Fractions**

Compare Fractions

Example 1: Compare $\frac{3}{4}$ and $\frac{7}{10}$.

① Find the LCD of the denominators 4 and 10:

$$4 = 2 \times 2$$
$$10 = 2 \times 5$$
$$LCD = 2 \times 2 \times 5 = 20$$

② Write equivalent fractions:

$$\frac{3}{4} \overset{\times 5}{\underset{\times 5}{=}} \frac{15}{20} \qquad \frac{7}{10} \overset{\times 2}{\underset{\times 2}{=}} \frac{14}{20}$$

③ Compare: $\frac{15}{20} > \frac{14}{20}$, or

$$\frac{3}{4} > \frac{7}{10}$$

Order Fractions

Example 2: Order from least to greatest: $\frac{2}{3}, \frac{5}{8}, \frac{3}{4}$.

① Find the LCD of the denominators 3, 8, and 4:

$$3 = 3$$
$$8 = 2 \times 2 \times 2$$
$$4 = 2 \times 2$$
$$LCD = 2 \times 2 \times 2 \times 3 = 24$$

② Write equivalent fractions:

$$\frac{2}{3} \overset{\times 8}{\underset{\times 8}{=}} \frac{16}{24} \qquad \frac{5}{8} \overset{\times 3}{\underset{\times 3}{=}} \frac{15}{24} \qquad \frac{3}{4} \overset{\times 6}{\underset{\times 6}{=}} \frac{18}{24}$$

③ Order:

15 , 16 , 18

$$\frac{15}{24} < \frac{16}{24} < \frac{18}{24}, \text{ or } \frac{5}{8} < \frac{2}{3} < \frac{3}{4}$$

Compare each pair of numbers using <, =, or >.

1. $\frac{2}{9}$ ☐ $\frac{1}{3}$ 2. $\frac{5}{6}$ ☐ $\frac{7}{8}$ 3. $\frac{7}{20}$ ☐ $\frac{3}{10}$

4. $\frac{3}{6}$ ☐ $\frac{4}{11}$ 5. $\frac{2}{3}$ ☐ $\frac{4}{6}$ 6. $\frac{4}{8}$ ☐ $\frac{2}{8}$

7. $\frac{3}{7}$ ☐ $\frac{5}{8}$ 8. $\frac{1}{3}$ ☐ $\frac{3}{9}$ 9. $\frac{1}{2}$ ☐ $\frac{3}{7}$

10. $\frac{4}{5}$ ☐ $\frac{7}{9}$ 11. $\frac{2}{3}$ ☐ $\frac{7}{10}$ 12. $2\frac{5}{9}$ ☐ $2\frac{3}{5}$

Order each set of numbers from least to greatest.

13. $\frac{3}{4}, \frac{5}{8}, \frac{1}{2}$ _____   14. $\frac{5}{8}, \frac{5}{6}, \frac{2}{3}$ _____   15. $\frac{1}{2}, \frac{5}{12}, \frac{2}{3}$ _____

16. $\frac{3}{5}, \frac{2}{3}, \frac{7}{12}$ _____   17. $\frac{1}{2}, \frac{3}{5}, \frac{3}{8}$ _____   18. $\frac{7}{8}, \frac{3}{4}, \frac{13}{16}$ _____

19. Suzanne swims $1\frac{1}{9}$ miles. Eugene swims $1\frac{5}{12}$ miles. Who swims farther? Show your work.

Practice 3-7

Compare each pair of numbers using <, =, or >.

1. $2\frac{14}{17}$ ☐ $1\frac{16}{17}$ 2. $\frac{15}{21}$ ☐ $\frac{5}{7}$ 3. $2\frac{7}{8}$ ☐ $2\frac{5}{6}$ 4. $1\frac{1}{2}$ ☐ $2\frac{1}{3}$

5. $3\frac{15}{16}$ ☐ $3\frac{21}{32}$ 6. $4\frac{7}{8}$ ☐ $3\frac{9}{10}$ 7. $5\frac{9}{10}$ ☐ $5\frac{18}{20}$ 8. $4\frac{7}{8}$ ☐ $5\frac{1}{8}$

9. $1\frac{19}{20}$ ☐ $2\frac{1}{20}$ 10. $4\frac{5}{6}$ ☐ $5\frac{19}{20}$ 11. $7\frac{3}{10}$ ☐ $7\frac{9}{30}$ 12. $2\frac{7}{15}$ ☐ $1\frac{14}{15}$

13. $4\frac{19}{24}$ ☐ $4\frac{7}{12}$ 14. $5\frac{19}{20}$ ☐ $6\frac{21}{22}$ 15. $4\frac{15}{20}$ ☐ $4\frac{21}{28}$ 16. $1\frac{2}{16}$ ☐ $1\frac{1}{4}$

Order each set of numbers from least to greatest.

17. $\frac{9}{10}, \frac{5}{6}, \frac{14}{15}$ 18. $1\frac{7}{8}, 1\frac{7}{12}, 1\frac{5}{6}$ 19. $\frac{14}{15}, \frac{9}{10}, \frac{11}{12}$

_____   _____   _____

20. $2\frac{1}{4}, 3\frac{7}{8}, 3\frac{5}{6}$ 21. $\frac{2}{3}, \frac{4}{5}, \frac{7}{30}, \frac{11}{15}$ 22. $2\frac{1}{6}, 1\frac{3}{4}, 3\frac{7}{8}, 2\frac{1}{10}$

_____   _____   _____

23. $\frac{5}{12}, \frac{17}{30}, \frac{3}{5}$ 24. $1\frac{5}{6}, 2\frac{1}{6}, 1\frac{11}{12}, 1\frac{11}{18}$ 25. $\frac{17}{20}, 1\frac{18}{25}, 2\frac{31}{36}$

_____   _____   _____

Use mental math to compare each pair of fractions using <, =, or >.

26. $\frac{1}{6}$ ☐ $\frac{1}{8}$ 27. $\frac{8}{9}$ ☐ $\frac{8}{12}$ 28. $\frac{1}{4}$ ☐ $\frac{1}{5}$

29. $\frac{3}{9}$ ☐ $\frac{3}{7}$ 30. $\frac{5}{50}$ ☐ $\frac{1}{60}$ 31. $\frac{9}{10}$ ☐ $\frac{10}{12}$

32. $\frac{1}{12}$ ☐ $\frac{1}{15}$ 33. $\frac{5}{6}$ ☐ $\frac{3}{4}$ 34. $\frac{1}{65}$ ☐ $\frac{3}{60}$

35. Four puppies measured $5\frac{1}{4}$ in., $5\frac{3}{8}$ in., $5\frac{5}{8}$ in., and $5\frac{5}{16}$ in. long at birth. Put the lengths in order from least to greatest.

_____

Reteaching 3-8

Example 1: Write 0.320 as a fraction in simplest form.

① Read. "320 thousandths"

② Write. $\frac{320}{1,000}$

③ Simplify. $\frac{320}{1,000} = \frac{320 \div 40}{1,000 \div 40} = \frac{8}{25}$

$$0.320 = \frac{8}{25}$$

Example 2: Write 6.95 as a mixed number in simplest form.

① Read. "6 and 95 hundredths"

② Write. $6\frac{95}{100}$

③ Simplify. $6\frac{95}{100} = 6\frac{19}{20}$

$$6.95 = 6\frac{19}{20}$$

Example 3: Write $\frac{1}{5}$ and $\frac{2}{3}$ as decimals.

Divide the numerator by the denominator. Insert zeros if needed.

$$\begin{array}{r} 0.2 \\ 5{\overline{)1.0}} \end{array} \qquad \begin{array}{r} 0.666\ldots \\ 3{\overline{)2.0000}} \\ -1\,8 \\ \hline 20 \\ -18 \\ \hline 2 \end{array}$$ ← The digits repeat because the remainder repeats.

$$\frac{1}{5} = 0.2 \qquad \frac{2}{3} = 0.666\ldots = 0.\overline{6}$$

0.2 is a *terminating decimal* because there is no remainder.

0.666 . . . is a repeating decimal because the remainder repeats. Write it as $0.\overline{6}$.

Write each decimal as a fraction or mixed number in simplest form.

1. 0.8 _____   **2.** 0.55 _____   **3.** 1.25 _____   **4.** 1.75 _____

5. 3.375 _____   **6.** 0.125 _____   **7.** 1.32 _____   **8.** 0.34 _____

9. 0.084 _____   **10.** 0.006 _____   **11.** 0.65 _____   **12.** 4.95 _____

Write each fraction or mixed number as a decimal.

13. $\frac{13}{20}$ _____   **14.** $\frac{1}{6}$ _____   **15.** $\frac{7}{20}$ _____   **16.** $2\frac{3}{5}$ _____

17. $\frac{19}{25}$ _____   **18.** $\frac{4}{9}$ _____   **19.** $\frac{7}{11}$ _____   **20.** $1\frac{5}{8}$ _____

21. $1\frac{2}{9}$ _____   **22.** $2\frac{2}{8}$ _____   **23.** $\frac{1}{25}$ _____   **24.** $\frac{5}{12}$ _____

State whether each fraction is less than, equal to, or greater than 0.50. Show your work.

25. $\frac{1}{3}$ _____   **26.** $\frac{20}{40}$ _____   **27.** $\frac{1}{6}$ _____

28. $\frac{7}{8}$ _____   **29.** $\frac{11}{13}$ _____   **30.** $\frac{8}{20}$ _____

Name _____ Class _____ Date _____

Practice 3-8

Write the decimal represented by each model as a fraction in simplest form.

1.

2.

3.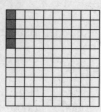

_____ _____ _____

Write each decimal as a fraction or mixed number in simplest form.

4. 0.6 _____ **5.** 1.25 _____ **6.** 0.74 _____ **7.** 0.29 _____

8. 0.635 _____ **9.** 0.8 _____ **10.** 6.16 _____ **11.** 0.95 _____

12. 0.645 _____ **13.** 0.782 _____ **14.** 0.493 _____ **15.** 0.758 _____

Write each fraction or mixed number as a decimal.

16. $\frac{5}{6}$ _____ **17.** $\frac{7}{8}$ _____ **18.** $\frac{9}{16}$ _____ **19.** $2\frac{4}{25}$ _____

20. $\frac{1}{12}$ _____ **21.** $1\frac{4}{15}$ _____ **22.** $\frac{9}{100}$ _____ **23.** $\frac{8}{9}$ _____

24. $\frac{7}{25}$ _____ **25.** $\frac{3}{50}$ _____ **26.** $\frac{1}{125}$ _____ **27.** $\frac{6}{11}$ _____

State whether each fraction is less than, equal to, or greater than 0.25.

28. $\frac{1}{3}$ _____ **29.** $\frac{3}{12}$ _____ **30.** $\frac{4}{9}$ _____

31. $\frac{2}{8}$ _____ **32.** $\frac{6}{15}$ _____ **33.** $\frac{4}{16}$ _____

34. $\frac{1}{10}$ _____ **35.** $\frac{9}{100}$ _____ **36.** $\frac{2}{10}$ _____

Determine whether each statement of equality is true or false.

37. $\frac{2}{6} = 0.33\bar{3}$ **38.** $0.4 = \frac{6}{15}$ **39.** $0.5 = \frac{8}{15}$

_____ _____ _____

40. $10.20 = 10\frac{2}{100}$ **41.** $4.3 = \frac{43}{10}$ **42.** $2\frac{4}{5} = 2.8$

_____ _____ _____

Reteaching 3-9

Lincoln Middle School needs new smoke alarms. The school has $415 to spend. Alarms with escape lights cost $18, and alarms with a false-alarm silencer cost $11. The school wants 4 times as many escape-light alarms as silencer alarms. How many of each kind can the school purchase?

Read and Understand

What facts are needed to solve the problem? *You need the costs of the alarms, $18 and $11; the amount to be spent, $415; and the fact that 4 times as many escape-light alarms as silencer alarms will be bought.*

Plan and Solve

You can try, check, and revise to solve this problem.

Try: Buy 12 escape-light alarms and 3 silencer alarms.

Check:
$$12 \times \$18 = \$216$$
$$3 \times \$11 = \underline{\$\ 33}$$
Add: $\$249$

$249 is a lot less than the $415 that the school has to spend. Revise with different combinations until you solve the problem.

Buy 20 escape-light alarms and 5 silencer alarms.

Check:
$$20 \times \$18 = \$360$$
$$5 \times \$11 = \underline{\$\ 55}$$
Add: $\$415$

Look Back and Check

Check to see whether your answer agrees with the information in the problem. *Is the total amount spent $415, or slightly less? Are there 4 times as many escape-light alarms as silencer alarms?*

Solve each problem by trying, checking, and revising.

1. Tina needs batteries. AA batteries cost $3 per pack. D batteries cost $4 per pack. If she has $26 to spend and buys 3 times as many packs of AA batteries as D batteries, how many packs of each does she buy?

2. Ian needs CDs for his CD burner. One package of 3 CDs sells for $5. Another pack of 2 costs $4. If Ian has $19 and buys 11 CDs, how many packs of each kind does he buy?

3. Hyugen has $50 to spend on CDs. New ones cost $9 and used ones cost $7. He wants to buy more new CDs than used. How many of each can he buy?

4. Frank has $41 to spend on computer disks. A pack of 10 ES brand disks costs $13, and a pack of 11 CW brand disks costs $14. How many packs of each can he buy if he spends all his money?

Practice 3-9

Solve each problem by trying, checking, and revising.

1. A deli sells ham sandwiches for $2 and roast beef sandwiches for $3. A group organizing a family reunion placed orders for 85 sandwiches. The bill came to $218 before tax. How many ham sandwiches were ordered?

    _____

2. Tickets for a community dinner cost $4 for adults and $3 for children. A total of 390 tickets was sold, earning $1,380. How many of each type of ticket were sold?

    _____

3. Place the digits 3, 4, 7, 9, and 12 in the circles at the right so that the product of these numbers is the same left to right and up and down. What is the product?

    _____

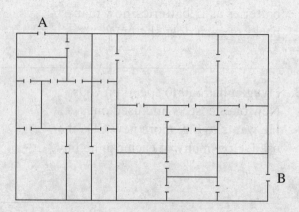

Choose a strategy to solve each problem.

4. Two numbers have a sum of 42 and a product of 432. What are the two numbers?

    _____

5. Two numbers have a sum of 70 and a product of 1,189. What are the two numbers?

    _____

6. Louise, Bill, and Fran each had a different piece of fruit packed in their lunches. An apple, an orange, and a banana were packed. Louise won't eat apples. Bill is allergic to oranges. Fran eats only bananas. What piece of fruit did each person have?

    _____

    _____

7. Paco joins a baseball card club. He brings 2 cards to the first meeting, 3 cards to the second meeting, 5 cards to the third meeting, and 8 cards to the fourth meeting. If he continues this pattern, how many cards will he bring to the fifth meeting?

    _____

8. The floor plan of the first floor of a museum is shown at the right. If you enter at A, is it possible to go through each doorway only one time, see each room, and exit at B? If this can be done, show how. You may enter each room more than one time.

    _____

    _____

Reteaching 4-1

Estimate sums and differences of fractions by using a benchmark. A *benchmark* is a number that is close to a fraction and is easy to use when you estimate.

Estimate: $\frac{4}{5} + \frac{3}{8}$ by using the benchmarks $0, \frac{1}{2},$ or 1.

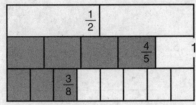

$\frac{4}{5} \approx 1$

$\frac{3}{8} \approx \frac{1}{2}$

$1 + \frac{1}{2} = 1\frac{1}{2}$

$\frac{4}{5} + \frac{3}{8} \approx 1\frac{1}{2}$

Estimate sums and differences of mixed numbers by rounding to the nearest whole number.

Subtract: $3\frac{1}{6} - 1\frac{9}{10}$

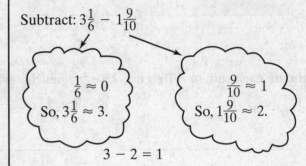

$3 - 2 = 1$

$3\frac{1}{6} - 1\frac{9}{10} \approx 1$

Estimate each sum or difference. Use the benchmarks $0, \frac{1}{2},$ and 1.

1. $\frac{7}{8} + \frac{1}{16}$ _____

2. $\frac{9}{10} + \frac{4}{5}$ _____

3. $\frac{15}{16} - \frac{1}{9}$ _____

4. $\frac{5}{8} - \frac{3}{7}$ _____

5. $\frac{21}{25} + \frac{1}{6}$ _____

6. $\frac{1}{2} + \frac{1}{18}$ _____

7. $\frac{4}{10} - \frac{2}{15}$ _____

8. $\frac{6}{7} + \frac{4}{5}$ _____

9. $\frac{7}{10} + \frac{3}{24}$ _____

10. $\frac{5}{9} + \frac{1}{15}$ _____

11. $\frac{1}{10} + \frac{1}{8}$ _____

12. $\frac{1}{18} + \frac{2}{10}$ _____

13. $\frac{6}{7} + \frac{2}{3}$ _____

14. $\frac{11}{12} - \frac{9}{10}$ _____

15. $\frac{13}{14} - \frac{4}{7}$ _____

16. $6\frac{1}{8} + 2\frac{9}{10}$ _____

17. $1\frac{1}{5} - \frac{9}{10}$ _____

18. $3\frac{8}{9} + 4\frac{8}{9}$ _____

19. $8\frac{1}{12} - \frac{8}{10}$ _____

20. $5\frac{8}{9} + 3\frac{2}{13}$ _____

21. $6\frac{9}{11} - 1\frac{1}{8}$ _____

22. $12\frac{7}{8} - \frac{11}{12}$ _____

23. $9\frac{7}{9} - \frac{9}{10}$ _____

24. $15\frac{3}{8} + 1\frac{1}{9}$ _____

25. $17\frac{2}{7} + \frac{8}{11}$ _____

26. $7\frac{1}{4} - \frac{15}{16}$ _____

27. $5\frac{1}{8} + \frac{13}{16}$ _____

Solve.

28. Katrina has a $7\frac{1}{2}$-foot roll of ribbon. She needs 2 strips of ribbon that each measure $3\frac{5}{6}$-feet long. Does she need more ribbon?

_____

29. Ricardo jogs $3\frac{3}{4}$ miles on Monday and $2\frac{1}{5}$ miles on Wednesday. Estimate the total number of miles he jogs.

_____

Practice 4-1

Write the fraction shown by each model. Then choose a benchmark for each measurement. Use $0, \frac{1}{2}$, or 1.

1.

   _____

2.

   _____

Estimate each sum or difference. Use the benchmarks $0, \frac{1}{2}$, and 1.

3. $\frac{5}{16} + \frac{5}{8}$

4. $\frac{10}{12} + \frac{4}{5}$

5. $\frac{8}{10} - \frac{1}{2}$

_____   _____   _____

6. $\frac{3}{4} + \frac{3}{8}$

7. $\frac{7}{10} - \frac{1}{6}$

8. $\frac{13}{15} - \frac{1}{12}$

_____   _____   _____

Estimate each sum or difference.

9. $4\frac{1}{4} - 1\frac{7}{9}$

10. $8\frac{6}{8} - 2\frac{1}{3}$

11. $5\frac{7}{8} + 3\frac{3}{4}$

_____   _____   _____

12. $8\frac{1}{12} - 3\frac{9}{10}$

13. $6\frac{5}{7} - 2\frac{2}{9}$

14. $3\frac{5}{8} + 2\frac{3}{10}$

_____   _____   _____

15. Name three fractions whose benchmark is $\frac{1}{2}$.

_____

16. Name three fractions whose benchmark is 1.

_____

17. The fabric for play costumes costs \$5.95 per yard. Patti needs $2\frac{7}{8}$ yards for one costume and $3\frac{5}{8}$ yards for another one. About how much will she spend on these costumes? Estimate the sum by first rounding to the nearest whole number.

_____

_____

18. One bag of oranges costs \$2.99 and weighs about $3\frac{7}{8}$ pounds. Individual oranges are sold at \$.89 per pound. Which is the better buy? Explain.

_____

_____

_____

Reteaching 4-2

Fractions With Like Denominators

Add: $\frac{1}{6} + \frac{3}{6}$

① Combine numerators over the denominator.

② Add numerators.

③ Simplify, if possible.

$\frac{1}{6} + \frac{3}{6} = \frac{1+3}{6}$

$= \frac{4}{6}$

$= \frac{2}{3}$

$\frac{1}{6} + \frac{3}{6} = \frac{2}{3}$

Subtract: $\frac{7}{10} - \frac{2}{10}$

① Combine numerators over the denominator.

② Subtract numerators.

③ Simplify, if possible.

$\frac{7}{10} - \frac{2}{10} = \frac{7-2}{10}$

$= \frac{5}{10}$

$= \frac{1}{2}$

$\frac{7}{10} - \frac{2}{10} = \frac{1}{2}$

Find each sum.

1. $\frac{1}{5} + \frac{3}{5}$ _____

2. $\frac{4}{6} + \frac{1}{6}$ _____

3. $\frac{3}{12} + \frac{3}{12}$ _____

4. $\frac{6}{10} + \frac{5}{10}$ _____

5. $\frac{3}{10} + \frac{2}{10}$ _____

6. $\frac{6}{12} + \frac{3}{12}$ _____

7. $\frac{5}{8} + \frac{1}{8}$ _____

8. $\frac{3}{8} + \frac{9}{8}$ _____

9. $\frac{3}{8} + \frac{6}{8}$ _____

Find each difference.

10. $\frac{6}{8} - \frac{3}{8}$ _____

11. $\frac{9}{10} - \frac{3}{10}$ _____

12. $\frac{3}{4} - \frac{1}{4}$ _____

13. $\frac{7}{12} - \frac{1}{12}$ _____

14. $\frac{8}{10} - \frac{6}{10}$ _____

15. $\frac{4}{6} - \frac{2}{6}$ _____

16. $\frac{5}{10} - \frac{1}{10}$ _____

17. $\frac{7}{12} - \frac{6}{12}$ _____

18. $\frac{9}{10} - \frac{4}{10}$ _____

Find each sum or difference.

19. $\frac{2}{7} + \frac{2}{7} - \frac{1}{7}$

20. $\frac{10}{100} + \frac{20}{100} + \frac{90}{100}$

21. $\frac{2}{5} - \frac{2}{5} + \frac{5}{5}$

_____

_____

_____

22. $\frac{10}{11} - \left(\frac{2}{11} + \frac{4}{11} \right)$

23. $\frac{8}{10} - \frac{2}{10} - \frac{1}{10}$

24. $\frac{62}{80} - \frac{10}{80} - \frac{5}{80}$

_____

_____

_____

25. For school photos, $\frac{1}{5}$ of the students choose to have a blue background, $\frac{2}{5}$ of the students choose to have a purple background, and $\frac{1}{5}$ of the students choose to have a gray background. What portion of the students choose to have another background color?

_____

Practice 4-2

Write each sum or difference in simplest form.

1. $\frac{1}{4} + \frac{2}{4}$

2. $\frac{7}{10} - \frac{4}{10}$

3. $\frac{5}{8} - \frac{3}{8}$

4. $\frac{1}{8} + \frac{5}{8}$

5. $\frac{5}{8} + \frac{2}{8}$

6. $\frac{3}{10} + \frac{6}{10}$

7. $\frac{11}{12} - \frac{5}{12}$

8. $\frac{11}{16} - \frac{3}{16}$

9. $\frac{3}{6} + \frac{1}{6}$

10. $\frac{7}{9} - \frac{3}{9}$

11. $\frac{11}{14} - \frac{3}{14}$

12. $\frac{5}{17} + \frac{13}{17}$

13. What is the total amount of sugar in the recipe at the right?

14. Martha decides to double the recipe. How much brown sugar will she use?

Martha's Cookie Recipe
1 cup shortening
2 eggs
$\frac{1}{4}$ cup white sugar
$\frac{1}{4}$ cup brown sugar
$1\frac{1}{2}$ cup flour
1 teaspoon vanilla

Estimate each sum or difference.

15. $\frac{3}{8} + \frac{2}{8} - \frac{4}{8}$

16. $\frac{1}{10} + \frac{2}{10} + \frac{4}{10}$

17. $\frac{7}{15} - \frac{2}{15} - \frac{5}{15}$

18. $\frac{9}{20} - \left(\frac{2}{20} - \frac{4}{20}\right)$

19. $\frac{6}{9} + \frac{2}{9} - \frac{1}{9}$

20. $\frac{12}{50} + \frac{20}{50} + \frac{8}{50}$

Solve.

21. At the tea shop, $\frac{5}{15}$ of the customers purchased green tea, $\frac{2}{15}$ of the customers purchased jasmine tea, and $\frac{5}{15}$ of the customers purchased herbal tea. What portion of the customers purchased another type of tea?

22. A piece of fabric is $\frac{7}{9}$ yard long. A piece of ribbon is $\frac{2}{9}$ yard long. How many more yards of ribbon do you need to have equal lengths of fabric and ribbon?

Reteaching 4-3

Fractions With Unlike Denominators

To add or subtract fractions with unlike denominators, you can use equivalent fractions.

Example 1: Find $\frac{5}{6} + \frac{1}{2}$.

① Find the least common denominator of 6 and 2.

The LCD is 6.

② Write equivalent fractions using the LCD.

$$\frac{5}{6} = \frac{5}{6} \qquad \frac{1}{2} = \frac{1 \times 3}{2 \times 3} = \frac{3}{6}$$

③ Add. Write the sum in simplest form.

$$\frac{5}{6} + \frac{1}{2} = \frac{5}{6} + \frac{3}{6}$$
$$= \frac{5+3}{6}$$
$$= \frac{8}{6}$$
$$= \frac{4}{3}$$
$$= 1\frac{1}{3}$$

$$\frac{5}{6} + \frac{1}{2} = 1\frac{1}{3}$$

Example 2: Find $\frac{4}{5} - \frac{1}{3}$.

① Find the least common denominator of 5 and 3.

The LCD is 15.

② Write equivalent fractions using the LCD.

$$\frac{4}{5} = \frac{4 \times 3}{5 \times 3} = \frac{12}{15} \qquad \frac{1}{3} = \frac{1 \times 5}{3 \times 5} = \frac{5}{15}$$

③ Subtract. Write the difference in simplest form.

$$\frac{4}{5} - \frac{1}{3} = \frac{12}{15} - \frac{5}{15}$$
$$= \frac{12-5}{15}$$
$$= \frac{7}{15}$$

$$\frac{4}{5} - \frac{1}{3} = \frac{7}{15}$$

Find each sum or difference.

1. $\frac{1}{2} + \frac{3}{4}$ _____

2. $\frac{11}{16} - \frac{5}{16}$ _____

3. $\frac{1}{6} + \frac{1}{3}$ _____

4. $\frac{7}{8} - \frac{1}{2}$ _____

5. $\frac{9}{10} + \frac{1}{2}$ _____

6. $\frac{2}{3} + \frac{5}{9}$ _____

7. $\frac{1}{2} + \frac{7}{10}$ _____

8. $\frac{3}{4} - \frac{5}{12}$ _____

9. $\frac{5}{8} + \frac{1}{4}$ _____

10. $\frac{15}{16} - \frac{1}{4}$ _____

11. $\frac{7}{12} - \frac{1}{3}$ _____

12. $\frac{5}{6} + \frac{1}{3}$ _____

13. $\frac{7}{8} - \frac{1}{4}$ _____

14. $\frac{3}{5} + \frac{1}{6}$ _____

15. $\frac{1}{12} + \frac{1}{10}$ _____

16. $\frac{7}{8} - \frac{3}{10}$ _____

17. $\frac{2}{6} + \frac{3}{4}$ _____

18. $\frac{3}{8} - \frac{1}{3}$ _____

19. $\frac{5}{8} + \frac{2}{3}$ _____

20. $\frac{3}{5} - \frac{1}{2}$ _____

21. $\frac{1}{8} + \frac{1}{5}$ _____

22. $\frac{7}{10} - \frac{3}{5}$ _____

23. $\frac{9}{10} - \frac{1}{2}$ _____

24. $\frac{1}{10} + \frac{4}{5}$ _____

Name _____ Class _____ Date _____

Practice 4-3

Fractions With Unlike Denominators

Write each sum or difference in simplest form.

1. $\frac{1}{4} + \frac{2}{3}$

_____

2. $\frac{2}{5} - \frac{1}{10}$

_____

3. $\frac{1}{6} + \frac{1}{4}$

_____

4. $\frac{5}{8} - \frac{1}{4}$

_____

5. $\frac{7}{8} - \frac{1}{2}$

_____

6. $\frac{3}{10} + \frac{4}{5}$

_____

7. $\frac{5}{6} - \frac{2}{5}$

_____

8. $\frac{5}{12} - \frac{1}{4}$

_____

9. $\frac{7}{16} + \frac{1}{8}$

_____

10. $\frac{11}{16} + \frac{5}{8}$

_____

11. $\frac{2}{7} + \frac{1}{2}$

_____

12. $\frac{4}{5} + \frac{3}{4}$

_____

13. $\frac{2}{3} - \frac{1}{6}$

_____

14. $\frac{2}{3} - \frac{5}{8}$

_____

15. $\frac{5}{7} + \frac{1}{5}$

_____

16. $\frac{3}{5} + \frac{7}{10}$

_____

17. Jeanie has a $\frac{3}{4}$-yard piece of ribbon. She needs one $\frac{3}{8}$-yard piece and one $\frac{1}{2}$-yard piece. Can she cut the piece of ribbon into the two smaller pieces? Explain.

_____

Simplify by using mental math.

18. $\frac{7}{10} + \frac{2}{5} - \frac{1}{10}$ _____

19. $\frac{5}{100} + \frac{20}{100} + \frac{30}{100}$ _____

20. $\frac{2}{8} - \frac{2}{4} + \frac{5}{8}$ _____

21. $\frac{10}{12} - \left(\frac{1}{12} + \frac{4}{6} \right)$ _____

22. $\frac{6}{10} - \frac{2}{10} + \frac{1}{2}$ _____

23. $\frac{8}{16} - \frac{1}{4} + \frac{8}{16}$ _____

24. For the class photo, $\frac{1}{5}$ of the students wore jeans, $\frac{2}{10}$ of the students wore shorts, and $\frac{4}{10}$ of the students wore a skirt. What portion of the students wore something else? _____

Reteaching 4-4

Adding Mixed Numbers

Some mixed numbers can be added mentally.

Example 1: Find $5\frac{1}{4} + 2\frac{1}{8}$.

① Add the whole numbers.

$$5 + 2 = 7$$

② Add the fractions.

$$\frac{1}{4} + \frac{1}{8} = \frac{2}{8} + \frac{1}{8} = \frac{3}{8}$$

③ Combine the two parts.

$$7 + \frac{3}{8} = 7\frac{3}{8}$$
$$5\frac{1}{4} + 2\frac{1}{8} = 7\frac{3}{8}$$

Or, you can follow these steps.

Example 2: Find $4\frac{4}{5} + 2\frac{9}{10}$.

① Write with a common denominator.

$$4\frac{4}{5} + 2\frac{9}{10} = 4\frac{8}{10} + 2\frac{9}{10}$$

② Add the whole numbers. $= 6\frac{17}{10}$
   Add the fractions.

③ Rename $6\frac{17}{10}$ as $7\frac{7}{10}$. $= 7\frac{7}{10}$

$$4\frac{4}{5} + 2\frac{9}{10} = 7\frac{7}{10}$$

Find each sum.

1. $4\frac{4}{7} + 1\frac{1}{7}$

2. $1\frac{1}{3} + 3\frac{1}{3}$

3. $2\frac{1}{2} + 4$

4. $8\frac{2}{5} + 4\frac{1}{10}$

5. $7\frac{3}{4} + 2\frac{1}{8}$

6. $2\frac{7}{10} + 3\frac{1}{5}$

7. $7\frac{2}{9} + 1\frac{4}{9}$

8. $8\frac{3}{14} + 2\frac{1}{7}$

9. $9\frac{3}{8} + 2\frac{1}{2}$

10. $1\frac{3}{4} + 4\frac{7}{8}$

11. $7\frac{2}{3} + 8\frac{5}{6}$

12. $1\frac{2}{5} + 9\frac{2}{3}$

13. $6\frac{3}{4} + 8\frac{4}{5}$

14. $3\frac{2}{3} + 5\frac{5}{6}$

15. $4\frac{2}{5} + 6\frac{7}{10}$

16. $6 + 3\frac{2}{5}$

17. $9\frac{1}{6} + 1\frac{1}{3}$

18. $8\frac{1}{16} + 4\frac{5}{8}$

Practice 4-4

Complete to rename each mixed number.

1. $3\frac{9}{8} = 4\frac{?}{8}$ _____

2. $5\frac{7}{4} = 6\frac{?}{4}$ _____

3. $2\frac{17}{12} = 3\frac{?}{12}$ _____

Write each sum in simplest form.

4. $4\frac{3}{10} + 5\frac{2}{5}$

5. $3\frac{7}{8} + 2\frac{1}{2}$

6. $5\frac{2}{3} + 3\frac{1}{4}$

7. $6\frac{3}{4} + 2\frac{1}{2}$

8. $1\frac{1}{12} + 3\frac{1}{6}$

9. $9\frac{2}{5} + 10\frac{3}{10}$

10. $7\frac{1}{3} + 5\frac{11}{12}$

11. $11\frac{7}{10} + 4$

12. $2\frac{2}{3} + 4\frac{3}{4}$

13. $7\frac{3}{4} + 2\frac{7}{8}$

14. $4\frac{1}{2} + 3\frac{5}{6}$

15. $7\frac{2}{3} + 1\frac{5}{6}$

16. $2\frac{1}{4} + 4\frac{3}{5}$

17. $5\frac{3}{8} + 7\frac{1}{4}$

18. $14\frac{5}{16} + 8\frac{3}{8}$

19. $\frac{11}{12} + 4\frac{5}{12}$

20. $27\frac{2}{5} + 3\frac{4}{5}$

21. $7\frac{1}{6} + 9\frac{7}{12}$

22. $22\frac{1}{4} + 3\frac{3}{5}$

23. $39\frac{1}{8} + 6\frac{3}{4}$

24. $14\frac{1}{16} + 3\frac{7}{8}$

25. $18\frac{1}{2} + 12\frac{1}{6}$

26. $80\frac{1}{10} + 5\frac{3}{5}$

27. $9\frac{3}{8} + 2\frac{1}{4}$

28. Estimate the length of rope needed to go around a triangle with sides $6\frac{1}{2}$ feet, $7\frac{3}{4}$ feet, and $10\frac{1}{4}$ feet.

_____

29. Sam grew three pumpkins for the pumpkin growing contest. The pumpkins weighed $24\frac{1}{8}$ pounds, $18\frac{2}{4}$ pounds, and $32\frac{5}{16}$ pounds. Find the combined total weight of Sam's pumpkins.

_____

Compare using <, =, or >. Use benchmarks to help.

30. $50\frac{7}{10} + 49\frac{1}{5}$ ☐ 100

31. $5\frac{3}{4} + 5\frac{1}{8}$ ☐ $11\frac{1}{2}$

32. $20\frac{1}{5} + 4\frac{9}{10}$ ☐ 25

33. $22\frac{1}{9} + 8\frac{3}{4}$ ☐ $30\frac{11}{12}$

34. $16\frac{6}{12} + 18\frac{4}{9}$ ☐ 34.5

35. $1\frac{1}{3} + 2\frac{1}{8}$ ☐ 3.5

Reteaching 4-5

Some mixed numbers can be subtracted mentally.

Example 1: Find $5\frac{2}{3} - 2\frac{1}{6}$.

① Subtract the whole numbers.

$$5 - 2 = 3$$

② Then, subtract the fractions.

$$\frac{2}{3} - \frac{1}{6} = \frac{4}{6} - \frac{1}{6} = \frac{3}{6} = \frac{1}{2}$$

③ Combine the two parts.

$$3 + \frac{1}{2} = 3\frac{1}{2}$$

$$5\frac{2}{3} - 2\frac{1}{6} = 3\frac{1}{2}$$

Sometimes you must *rename* the first fraction before subtracting.

Example 2: Find $6\frac{1}{2} - 2\frac{3}{4}$.

① Write with a common denominator.

$$6\frac{1}{2} - 2\frac{3}{4} = 6\frac{2}{4} - 2\frac{3}{4}$$

② Rename $6\frac{2}{4}$. $\qquad = 5\frac{6}{4} - 2\frac{3}{4}$

③ Subtract the whole numbers. $\quad = 3\frac{3}{4}$
Then, subtract the fractions.
Simplify, if necessary.

$$6\frac{1}{2} - 2\frac{3}{4} = 3\frac{3}{4}$$

Find each difference.

1. $7\frac{7}{10} - 2\frac{3}{10}$

2. $3\frac{3}{4} - 1\frac{1}{2}$

3. $6\frac{2}{3} - 2\frac{1}{6}$

_____

_____

_____

4. $9\frac{7}{8} - 7\frac{3}{4}$

5. $8\frac{1}{2} - 3\frac{1}{4}$

6. $14\frac{1}{3} - 8\frac{1}{4}$

_____

_____

_____

7. $12\frac{1}{3} - 9\frac{2}{3}$

8. $6\frac{5}{8} - 2\frac{3}{4}$

9. $7\frac{5}{7} - 4\frac{13}{14}$

_____

_____

_____

10. $10\frac{2}{3} - 7\frac{5}{6}$

11. $5\frac{7}{16} - 1\frac{1}{2}$

12. $8\frac{2}{5} - 3\frac{2}{3}$

_____

_____

_____

13. $6\frac{1}{8} - 3\frac{1}{16}$

14. $9\frac{5}{12} - 5\frac{3}{4}$

15. $12\frac{3}{4} - 6\frac{1}{8}$

_____

_____

_____

16. $7\frac{2}{5} - 2\frac{1}{4}$

17. $15\frac{5}{12} - 8\frac{1}{3}$

18. $4\frac{1}{10} - 2\frac{4}{5}$

_____

_____

_____

Practice 4-5

Write each difference in simplest form.

1. $10\frac{11}{16} - 3\frac{7}{8}$ _____

2. $8\frac{1}{3} - 2\frac{3}{8}$ _____

3. $9 - 3\frac{2}{5}$ _____

4. $5\frac{3}{16} - 2\frac{3}{8}$ _____

5. $8\frac{1}{6} - 3\frac{2}{5}$ _____

6. $7\frac{1}{2} - 3$ _____

7. $2\frac{3}{4} - 1\frac{1}{8}$ _____

8. $4\frac{1}{8} - 2\frac{1}{16}$ _____

9. $9\frac{2}{3} - 3\frac{5}{6}$ _____

10. $2\frac{1}{10} - 1\frac{2}{5}$ _____

11. $15\frac{7}{12} - 8\frac{1}{2}$ _____

12. $6\frac{7}{16} - 2\frac{7}{8}$ _____

13. $27\frac{1}{4} - 13\frac{11}{12}$ _____

14. $5\frac{2}{5} - 1\frac{1}{4}$ _____

15. $10\frac{2}{3} - 7\frac{3}{4}$ _____

16. $5\frac{3}{4} - 2\frac{1}{2}$ _____

17. $16\frac{5}{12} - 10\frac{1}{3}$ _____

18. $23\frac{7}{8} - 9\frac{1}{16}$ _____

19. $35\frac{1}{2} - 32\frac{1}{5}$ _____

20. $25\frac{1}{3} - 17\frac{3}{4}$ _____

21. $33\frac{1}{2} - 27\frac{1}{10}$ _____

22. $24\frac{3}{8} - 18\frac{5}{6}$ _____

23. $12\frac{3}{8} - 8\frac{3}{16}$ _____

24. $9\frac{1}{4} - 5\frac{1}{2}$ _____

Solve.

25. Robbie needs to buy fencing for his square vegetable garden that measures $16\frac{3}{4}$ feet on a side. One side borders the back of the garage. The fencing costs $4 per feet. Estimate how much the fencing will cost.

_____

26. Paula has 2 yards of elastic. One project needs a piece $\frac{3}{4}$ yard. Does she have enough for another project that needs $1\frac{1}{3}$ yards? Explain.

_____

_____

27. Use a ruler or measuring tape to find the perimeter of your desk. Measure to the nearest half inch.

width:_____ length:_____ perimeter:_____

Now find the perimeter of your teacher's desk.

width:_____ length:_____ perimeter:_____

Subtract to find the difference in the perimeters. _____

Name _____ Class _____ Date _____

Reteaching 4-6

You can use mental math to solve addition and subtraction equations that involve fractions or mixed numbers. To solve equations involving fractions with unlike denominators, you need to change the fractions to equivalent fractions with like denominators.

Solve $x - \frac{3}{8} = \frac{5}{16}$.

$$x - \frac{3}{8} = \frac{5}{16}$$

$\underline{+ \frac{3}{8} \quad + \frac{3}{8}}$ Add $\frac{3}{8}$ to each side.

$x = \frac{5}{16} + \frac{3}{8}$ Write the sum.

$= \frac{5}{16} + \frac{6}{16}$ The LCD is 16. Write $\frac{3}{8}$ as $\frac{6}{16}$.

$= \frac{11}{16}$ Simplify.

Solve each equation.

1. $x + \frac{1}{5} = \frac{4}{5}$

What number plus $\frac{1}{5}$ equals $\frac{4}{5}$? _____ So, $x =$ _____.

Show that the equation is true. _____

2. $x - \frac{1}{3} = \frac{2}{9}$

What is the least common multiple of 3 and 9? _____

Rewrite the equation using like denominators. _____

What number minus $\frac{3}{9}$ equals $\frac{2}{9}$? _____ So, $x =$ _____.

Show that the equation is true. _____

Solve each equation.

3. $\frac{1}{4} + x = \frac{3}{4}$ $x =$ _____

4. $y - \frac{5}{8} = \frac{1}{8}$ $y =$ _____

5. $\frac{7}{10} - c = \frac{2}{5}$ $c =$ _____

6. $\frac{5}{12} + r = \frac{7}{3}$ $r =$ _____

7. $\frac{1}{12} + b = \frac{1}{4}$ $b =$ _____

8. $s - \frac{1}{2} = \frac{1}{6}$ $s =$ _____

9. $d + \frac{1}{3} = \frac{7}{12}$ $d =$ _____

10. $\frac{5}{6} - f = \frac{7}{12}$ $f =$ _____

11. $s + \frac{3}{8} = \frac{3}{4}$ $s =$ _____

12. $t - \frac{3}{10} = \frac{5}{8}$ $t =$ _____

Practice 4-6

Solve each equation using mental math. Write your solution in simplest form.

1. $\frac{5}{17} + x = \frac{8}{17}$

_____

2. $\frac{2}{7} + x = \frac{5}{7}$

_____

3. $x - \frac{1}{2} = \frac{1}{10}$

_____

4. $\frac{7}{8} - x = \frac{13}{16}$

_____

5. $\frac{4}{7} - x = \frac{6}{35}$

_____

6. $x - \frac{1}{5} = \frac{3}{10}$

_____

7. $x + \frac{7}{22} = \frac{13}{22}$

_____

8. $\frac{7}{9} - x = \frac{1}{36}$

_____

9. $x - \frac{1}{6} = \frac{1}{6}$

_____

10. $x + \frac{1}{4} = \frac{7}{16}$

_____

11. $\frac{5}{6} + x = \frac{17}{18}$

_____

12. $\frac{3}{8} - x = \frac{1}{24}$

_____

Write and solve an equation for each situation.

13. Lori and Fraz ate $\frac{7}{12}$ of a vegetable pizza. If Lori ate $\frac{1}{3}$ of the pizza, how much of it did Fraz eat?

_____

14. Irene's gas tank was $\frac{9}{10}$ full when she left her house, and it was $\frac{7}{15}$ full when she arrived for her vacation. What fraction of a tank of gas did she use driving there?

_____

15. Last year, Wyatt weighed $74\frac{1}{8}$ pounds at football camp. When he weighed in this year, he was $4\frac{5}{12}$ pounds heavier. How much does Wyatt currently weigh?

_____

16. Nora bought 3 bottles of juice for a picnic. After the picnic she had $\frac{3}{8}$ bottle left. How much juice did Nora and her friends drink?

_____

Reteaching 4-7

Find the elapsed time between 6:15 A.M. and 11:10 A.M.

1. Set up as subtraction.

$$11:10$$
$$-6:15$$

2. Rename 11:10 as 10:70.

$$11:10 \rightarrow 10:70$$
$$-6:15 \rightarrow -6:15$$

3. Subtract.

$$10:70$$
$$-6:15$$
$$\overline{\quad 4:55}$$

The elapsed time is 4 hours 55 minutes.

You can find elapsed time from a schedule.

Leave	Arrive
Boston 7:09 A.M.	New York 11:02 A.M.

For travel time, find the elapsed time between 7:09 A.M. and 11:02 A.M.

$11:02 - 7:09 = 3$ hours 53 minutes

For each time, write an equivalent time using only the smaller unit.

Example: 4 hours 55 minutes = $4 \times 60 + 55 = 295$ minutes

1. 3 hours 25 minutes

_____

2. 2 hours 17 minutes

_____

3. 2 hours 48 minutes

_____

4. 5 hours 18 minutes

_____

5. 6 hours 13 minutes

_____

6. 5 hours 39 minutes

_____

Find the elapsed time between each pair of times.

7. 6:45 P.M. and 9:20 P.M.

_____

8. 9:36 A.M. and 11:50 A.M.

_____

9. 5:45 A.M. and 11:30 A.M.

_____

10. 3:11 P.M. and 10:40 P.M.

_____

11. 8:15 A.M. and 10:09 P.M.

_____

12. 1:00 A.M. and 7:28 P.M.

_____

Use the schedule to answer the following questions.

13. How much time do you have to get to the game?

_____

Leave for game	6:15 P.M.
Game begins	7:35 P.M.
Game ends	10:20 P.M.

14. How long is the game?

_____

Practice 4-7

Clark is trying to plan his Saturday. He estimates each activity will take the following times.

Make a schedule for Clark's day if he wakes up at 7:00 A.M. Assume all his activities are done in the given order.

	Activity	Amount of Time	Time of Day
1.	Get up, eat breakfast	30 min	_____
2.	Mow lawn	1 h	_____
3.	Rake yard	2 h	_____
4.	Wash, wax car	45 min	_____
5.	Walk dog	15 min	_____
6.	Clean room	45 min	_____
7.	Eat lunch	30 min	_____
8.	Shop for school clothes	1 h 30 min	_____
9.	Read book	45 min	_____
10.	Do homework	1 h 15 min	_____
11.	Baby-sit brother	2 h	_____
12.	Eat supper	45 min	_____
13.	Get ready for party	30 min	_____
14.	Ride to party	20 min	_____
15.	Party	2 h	_____
16.	Ride home	20 min	_____

Find the elapsed time between each pair of times.

17. from 2:12 P.M. to 10:18 P.M.

_____

18. from 9:35 A.M. to 8:48 P.M

_____

19. from 6:45 P.M. to 11:24 A.M.

_____

20. from 2:55 A.M. to 8:13 A.M.

_____

21. from 7:00 P.M. to 8:56 P.M.

_____

22. from 8:22 P.M. to 11:47 A.M.

_____

23. The movie begins at 7:45 P.M. and lets out at 10:20 P.M. How long is the movie?

_____

24. A plane left at 10:45 A.M. and landed at 4:37 P.M. How long was the flight?

_____

Reteaching 4-8

Yori found that each time a ball bounces, it returns to one half its previous height. If she drops the ball from 40 feet, how many feet will it have traveled when it hits the ground the fourth time?

Read and Understand

What does the problem ask?
Find the total distance the ball will travel up and down by the time it hits the ground the fourth time.

Plan and Solve

You can draw a diagram. How many feet will the first segment represent?
The first segment will represent 40 feet.

Draw a diagram to represent the problem.

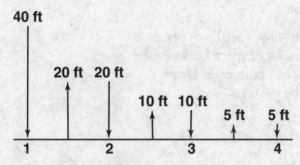

Add to solve. $40 + 20 + 20 + 10 + 10 + 5 + 5 = 110$ feet

Look Back and Check

How can you be sure that the solution solves the problem?
Count the number of times the ball hits the ground; check that each bounce is one half the height of the previous bounce.

Solve each problem by drawing a diagram.

1. Yori drops a ball from 64 feet. How far will it travel until it hits the ground the fourth time if it also returns to one half the height of its previous bounce?

   _____

2. Yori drops a ball from the same height in Exercise 1. She allows it to bounce 4 times before stopping it. If it returns to $\frac{1}{4}$ its dropped height, how much less will it travel than the ball in Exercise 1?

   _____

3. A ball returns to one half its dropped height. By the time it hits the ground the fourth time, it has traveled 66 feet. From what height was it dropped?

   _____

4. When a ball bounces, it returns to a height $\frac{3}{4}$ its previous height. After it hits the ground the second time, it bounces up 9 feet. From what height was it dropped?

   _____

Practice 4-8

Frank is laying square tiles on a rectangular floor. He wants the perimeter tiles to be a different color for two rows around the edges of the room. The dimensions of the room are 20 feet by 10 feet. Each tile is 1 foot on a side.

1. Draw a diagram to show how Frank could tile the floor. Use two colors.

2. How many border tiles does he need?

   _____

3. How many inside tiles does he need?

   _____

Solve each problem by drawing a diagram.

4. Jessica is hanging five posters on a 19-foot wall. Each poster is 2 feet wide, and she wants to have 1 foot of space between the posters and an equal amount of space at both ends. Draw a diagram to show the placement of the posters.

5. Suppose you are hanging posters along a 35-foot wall in the hallway. Each poster is 2 feet wide.

   a. What is the greatest number of posters that you could fit along the wall without overlap?

   _____

   b. What is the greatest number of posters that you could fit along the wall if you kept 2 feet between them? Draw a diagram to show your answer.

Choose a strategy to solve each problem.

6. Matthew earns $.10 for each local newspaper he delivers twice a week. His brother earns $.25 for delivering each Sunday newspaper. They deliver papers to the same number of houses and together they earn $13.95 per week. How many papers does each boy deliver each week?

   _____

7. Megan's car averaged 336 miles on 12 gallons of gas. How many gallons of gas did Megan use to drive 1,344 miles on vacation?

   _____

Reteaching 5-1

You can model $\frac{2}{3}$ of $\frac{1}{4}$.

① Show $\frac{1}{4}$.

② Divide into thirds.

③ Shade $\frac{2}{3}$ of the $\frac{1}{4}$.

$$\frac{2}{3} \text{ of } \frac{1}{4} = \frac{2}{12} = \frac{1}{6}$$

Or you can use multiplication.

$$\frac{2}{3} \text{ of } \frac{1}{4} = \frac{2}{3} \times \frac{1}{4}$$

$$= \frac{2 \times 1}{3 \times 4}$$

$$= \frac{2}{12}$$

$$= \frac{1}{6}$$

Write the multiplication problem each model represents.

1.

_____

2.

_____

Find each product.

3. $\frac{1}{9}$ of $\frac{2}{3}$

4. $\frac{2}{7} \times \frac{1}{2}$

5. $\frac{5}{8} \cdot 6$

6. $\frac{3}{4} \cdot \frac{4}{7}$

_____ _____ _____ _____

7. $\frac{7}{10}$ of $\frac{1}{3}$

8. $\frac{5}{6} \times \frac{3}{4}$

9. $\frac{3}{8}$ of $\frac{7}{10}$

10. $\frac{3}{4} \times \frac{1}{9}$

_____ _____ _____ _____

11. $\frac{2}{9}$ of 8

12. $\frac{1}{3}$ of 2

13. $\frac{5}{9}$ of 4

14. $\frac{3}{4} \cdot \frac{2}{5}$

_____ _____ _____ _____

15. Every day you eat $\frac{1}{4}$ cup of cereal. Your brother eats 5 times as much. How many cups of cereal does your brother eat? _____

Practice 5-1

Multiplying Fractions

Draw a model to find each product.

1. $\frac{1}{6} \times \frac{3}{4}$

2. $\frac{2}{5} \times \frac{1}{2}$

Find each product.

3. $\frac{3}{5}$ of 10

4. $\frac{1}{4}$ of 12

5. $\frac{2}{3}$ of 6

6. $\frac{4}{5}$ of $\frac{5}{8}$

_____

_____

_____

_____

7. $\frac{5}{6}$ of $\frac{3}{8}$

8. $\frac{3}{5}$ of $\frac{1}{2}$

9. $\frac{3}{4}$ of 12

10. $\frac{2}{5}$ of 15

_____

_____

_____

_____

11. $\frac{3}{16}$ of 8

12. $\frac{1}{2} \times \frac{5}{6}$

13. $\frac{3}{4} \times \frac{7}{8}$

14. $\frac{1}{3}$ of $\frac{2}{5}$

_____

_____

_____

_____

15. $\frac{3}{5}$ of $\frac{3}{4}$

16. $\frac{1}{2} \cdot \frac{1}{3}$

17. $\frac{1}{8} \times \frac{3}{4}$

18. $\frac{2}{5} \times \frac{7}{11}$

_____

_____

_____

_____

19. $\frac{2}{3}$ of $\frac{1}{4}$

20. $\frac{2}{5} \cdot \frac{1}{2}$

21. $\frac{1}{4}$ of $\frac{4}{5}$

22. $\frac{5}{6} \cdot \frac{2}{5}$

_____

_____

_____

_____

23. $\frac{2}{7}$ of $\frac{3}{5}$

24. $\frac{1}{3}$ of $\frac{9}{10}$

25. $\frac{1}{12} \times \frac{3}{4}$

26. $\frac{3}{10} \cdot \frac{3}{5}$

_____

_____

_____

_____

27. What product does the model represent?

_____

Solve.

28. A kitten eats $\frac{1}{4}$ cup of cat food. Another cat in the same
household eats 6 times as much. How much food does the cat eat?

_____

29. You brought home $\frac{1}{2}$ of a can of paint. You then used $\frac{2}{3}$ of the
paint to cover a table top. What fraction of a full can of paint did
you use?

_____

Reteaching 5-2

Multiplying Mixed Numbers

Example 1: Multiply: $2\frac{1}{7} \times 2\frac{2}{5}$

① Change to improper fractions. $\frac{15}{7} \times \frac{12}{5}$

② Simplify. $\overset{3}{\frac{15}{7}} \times \frac{12}{\underset{1}{5}}$

③ Multiply. $\frac{36}{7} \leftarrow 3 \times 12$
$\phantom{\frac{36}{7}} \leftarrow 7 \times 1$

④ Simplify. $5\frac{1}{7}$

$2\frac{1}{7} \times 2\frac{2}{5} = 5\frac{1}{7}$

Example 2: Multiply: $\frac{2}{3} \times 5\frac{1}{4}$

$\frac{2}{3} \times \frac{21}{4}$

$\overset{1}{\underset{1}{\frac{2}{3}}} \times \overset{7}{\underset{2}{\frac{21}{4}}}$

$\frac{7}{2} \leftarrow 1 \times 7$
$\phantom{\frac{7}{2}} \leftarrow 1 \times 2$

$3\frac{1}{2}$

$\frac{2}{3} \times 5\frac{1}{4} = 3\frac{1}{2}$

Find each product.

1. $1\frac{1}{4} \times 2\frac{2}{3}$

2. $2\frac{2}{5} \times 4\frac{1}{2}$

3. $3\frac{1}{7} \times 2\frac{4}{5}$

4. $\frac{1}{5} \times 2\frac{7}{9}$

5. $12\frac{1}{2} \times 2\frac{2}{5}$

6. $2\frac{1}{8} \times 2\frac{2}{3}$

7. $5\frac{1}{3} \times 1\frac{7}{8}$

8. $\frac{1}{2} \times 3\frac{3}{5}$

9. $2\frac{1}{7} \times 4\frac{2}{3}$

10. $1\frac{1}{2} \times 2\frac{6}{7}$

11. $1\frac{5}{6} \times 2\frac{1}{4}$

12. $5\frac{1}{4} \times 2\frac{2}{7}$

13. $\frac{1}{4} \times 1\frac{3}{5}$

14. $\frac{1}{7} \times 1\frac{3}{4}$

15. $\frac{2}{9} \times 2\frac{1}{4}$

16. $3\frac{1}{3} \times 3\frac{3}{10}$

17. $1\frac{2}{3} \times 3\frac{1}{2}$

18. $1\frac{2}{5} \times 4\frac{1}{3}$

19. $\frac{1}{7} \times 1\frac{3}{5}$

20. $\frac{3}{5} \times 8\frac{1}{2}$

21. $3\frac{2}{5} \times 2\frac{1}{2}$

22. $1\frac{2}{3} \times 7\frac{1}{2}$

23. $1\frac{3}{10} \times 2\frac{6}{7}$

24. $\frac{3}{16} \times 1\frac{1}{7}$

25. $2\frac{6}{7} \times 1\frac{2}{5}$

Solve.

26. Estimate the area of a window pane that has dimensions $6\frac{1}{8}$ by $11\frac{1}{4}$ inches.

27. A hamster is $2\frac{1}{2}$ inches long. A rabbit is $3\frac{1}{2}$ times as long as the hamster. How long is the rabbit?

Practice 5-2

Estimate each product.

1. $2\frac{5}{6} \times 1\frac{3}{4}$ _____

2. $3\frac{3}{8} \times 7\frac{1}{4}$ _____

3. $5\frac{3}{8} \times 2\frac{7}{8}$ _____

4. $2\frac{3}{8} \times 4\frac{4}{5}$ _____

5. $6\frac{7}{12} \times 5\frac{9}{10}$ _____

6. $7\frac{1}{3} \times 10\frac{11}{12}$ _____

7. $12\frac{1}{4} \times 3\frac{3}{4}$ _____

8. $8\frac{1}{6} \times 2\frac{1}{4}$ _____

9. $15\frac{2}{3} \times 5\frac{5}{7}$ _____

Find each product.

10. $2\frac{5}{6} \times 1\frac{3}{4}$ _____

11. $3\frac{3}{8} \times 7\frac{1}{4}$ _____

12. $5\frac{3}{8} \times 2\frac{7}{8}$ _____

13. $2\frac{3}{8} \times 4\frac{4}{5}$ _____

14. $6\frac{7}{12} \times 5\frac{9}{10}$ _____

15. $7\frac{1}{3} \times 10\frac{11}{12}$ _____

16. $12\frac{1}{4} \times 3\frac{3}{4}$ _____

17. $8\frac{1}{6} \times 2\frac{1}{4}$ _____

18. $15\frac{2}{3} \times 5\frac{5}{7}$ _____

19. $\frac{1}{4} \times 5\frac{2}{5}$ _____

20. $2\frac{3}{8} \times \frac{4}{5}$ _____

21. $1\frac{1}{2} \times 5\frac{1}{3}$ _____

22. $3\frac{3}{8} \times 6$ _____

23. $\frac{3}{4} \times 1\frac{3}{5}$ _____

24. $9\frac{3}{5} \times \frac{1}{3}$ _____

25. $1\frac{1}{4} \times 2\frac{2}{3}$ _____

26. $1\frac{3}{5} \times \frac{1}{4}$ _____

27. $6\frac{1}{4} \times 1\frac{2}{5}$ _____

28. $\frac{7}{8} \times 3\frac{1}{5}$ _____

29. $5\frac{1}{3} \times 2\frac{1}{4}$ _____

30. $\frac{3}{5} \times 4\frac{1}{2}$ _____

31. $\frac{5}{8} \times 7\frac{3}{5}$ _____

32. $5\frac{1}{3} \times \frac{5}{8}$ _____

33. $2\frac{4}{5} \times \frac{3}{7}$ _____

34. $3\frac{1}{3} \times 3\frac{3}{10}$ _____

35. $5\frac{1}{2} \times \frac{2}{5}$ _____

36. $1\frac{2}{3} \times 3\frac{3}{4}$ _____

Solve.

37. Ken used a piece of lumber to build a bookshelf. If he made three shelves that are each $2\frac{1}{2}$ ft long, how long was the piece of lumber? _____

38. Deanna's cake recipe needs to be doubled for a party. How much of each ingredient should Deanna use?

Cake Recipe		
ingredient	*amount*	*doubled amount*
flour	$2\frac{1}{4}$ cups	_____
sugar	$1\frac{3}{4}$ cups	_____
butter	$1\frac{1}{2}$ cups	_____
milk	$\frac{3}{4}$ cup	_____

Name _____ Class _____ Date _____

Reteaching 5-3

Find $8 \div \frac{4}{5}$.

① The *reciprocal* of $\frac{4}{5}$ is $\frac{5}{4}$.

$$\frac{4}{5} \diagdown \frac{5}{4}$$

② Multiply 8 by the reciprocal.

$$8 \div \frac{4}{5} = 8 \times \frac{5}{4} = \frac{{}^2 \cancel{8}}{1} \times \frac{5}{\cancel{4}_1} = \frac{2 \times 5}{1 \times 1} = 10$$

$$8 \div \frac{4}{5} = 10$$

Find $\frac{4}{9} \div \frac{8}{15}$.

① The *reciprocal* of $\frac{8}{15}$ is $\frac{15}{8}$.

$$\frac{8}{15} \diagdown \frac{15}{8}$$

② Multiply $\frac{4}{9}$ by the reciprocal.

$$\frac{4}{9} \div \frac{8}{15} = \frac{4}{9} \times \frac{15}{8} = \frac{{}^1\cancel{4}}{{}_3\cancel{9}} \times \frac{\cancel{15}^5}{\cancel{8}_2} = \frac{1 \times 5}{3 \times 2} = \frac{5}{6}$$

$$\frac{4}{9} \div \frac{8}{15} = \frac{5}{6}$$

Write the reciprocal of each number.

1. $\frac{1}{4}$ _____

2. $\frac{5}{3}$ _____

3. $\frac{1}{20}$ _____

4. $\frac{8}{9}$ _____

5. 14 _____

6. 18 _____

7. $\frac{5}{9}$ _____

8. $\frac{3}{11}$ _____

9. $\frac{9}{7}$ _____

10. $\frac{11}{12}$ _____

11. $\frac{2}{7}$ _____

12. $\frac{3}{15}$ _____

Find each quotient.

13. $2 \div \frac{2}{3}$ _____

14. $7 \div \frac{7}{8}$ _____

15. $9 \div \frac{3}{4}$ _____

16. $6 \div \frac{2}{5}$ _____

17. $5 \div \frac{2}{3}$ _____

18. $14 \div \frac{5}{6}$ _____

19. $\frac{4}{5} \div \frac{4}{7}$ _____

20. $\frac{7}{8} \div \frac{7}{9}$ _____

21. $\frac{4}{7} \div 2$ _____

22. $\frac{7}{8} \div \frac{2}{3}$ _____

23. $\frac{1}{2} \div 4$ _____

24. $\frac{2}{5} \div \frac{3}{4}$ _____

25. $\frac{9}{10} \div 3$ _____

26. $\frac{3}{5} \div 5$ _____

27. $\frac{5}{8} \div 10$ _____

28. $\frac{3}{4} \div \frac{7}{8}$ _____

29. $\frac{5}{6} \div \frac{1}{3}$ _____

30. $\frac{11}{12} \div \frac{3}{4}$ _____

Practice 5-3

Write the reciprocal of each number.

1. $\frac{7}{10}$ _____

2. 4 _____

3. $\frac{1}{3}$ _____

4. $\frac{1}{12}$ _____

5. Draw a diagram to show how many $\frac{3}{4}$-ft pieces of string can be cut from a piece of string $4\frac{1}{2}$ ft long.

Find each quotient.

6. $\frac{3}{10} \div \frac{4}{5}$ _____

7. $\frac{3}{8} \div 3$ _____

8. $\frac{1}{3} \div \frac{2}{7}$ _____

9. $\frac{1}{4} \div \frac{1}{4}$ _____

10. $\frac{7}{8} \div \frac{2}{7}$ _____

11. $\frac{1}{4} \div \frac{1}{8}$ _____

12. $\frac{1}{2} \div \frac{2}{5}$ _____

13. $\frac{8}{9} \div \frac{1}{2}$ _____

14. $3 \div \frac{3}{8}$ _____

Solve.

15. How many $\frac{3}{4}$-cup servings are there in a 6-cup package of rice?

_____

16. George cut 5 oranges into quarters. How many pieces of orange did he have?

_____

17. A cake recipe calls for $\frac{5}{8}$ cup of butter. One tablespoon equals $\frac{1}{16}$ cup. How many tablespoons of butter are used to make the cake?

_____

18. Maureen, Frank, Tashia, Zane, Eric, and Wesley are addressing envelopes for volunteer work at a local charity. They were given $\frac{3}{4}$ of an entire mailing to address to be evenly divided among six of them. What fraction of the entire mailing does each person address?

_____

19. Study the tangram pieces at the right. If the entire square is 1, find the fractional value of each piece. You can copy the tangram and cut the pieces to compare them.

Reteaching 5-4

Example 1: Estimate $36\frac{1}{3} \div 5\frac{7}{8}$.

$36\frac{1}{3} \div 5\frac{7}{8}$ Round mixed numbers to nearest whole number.

$36 \div 6 = 6$ Find the quotient of the rounded values.

Example 2: Find $5\frac{1}{3} \div 2\frac{2}{5}$.

1. Write each mixed number as an improper fraction.

$$5\frac{1}{3} \div 2\frac{2}{5} = \frac{16}{3} \div \frac{12}{5}$$

2. The *reciprocal* of $\frac{12}{5}$ is $\frac{5}{12}$.

$$\frac{12}{5} \diagdown \frac{5}{12}$$

3. Multiply $\frac{16}{3}$ by the reciprocal.

$$\frac{16}{3} \div \frac{12}{5} = \frac{\overset{4}{16}}{3} \times \frac{5}{\underset{3}{12}} = \frac{4 \times 5}{3 \times 3} = \frac{20}{9} = 2\frac{2}{9}$$

$$5\frac{1}{3} \div 2\frac{2}{5} = 2\frac{2}{9}$$

Estimate each quotient.

1. $14\frac{8}{9} \div 5\frac{1}{5}$ _____

2. $19\frac{2}{3} \div 3\frac{8}{9}$ _____

3. $50\frac{2}{3} \div 2\frac{6}{7}$ _____

4. $5\frac{1}{3} \div 2\frac{2}{3}$ _____

5. $6\frac{1}{4} \div 2\frac{1}{2}$ _____

6. $9 \div 3\frac{1}{3}$ _____

7. $12 \div 6\frac{1}{2}$ _____

8. $5 \div 1\frac{1}{5}$ _____

9. $2\frac{7}{10} \div \frac{4}{5}$ _____

10. $6\frac{1}{2} \div 2\frac{1}{6}$ _____

11. $5\frac{2}{3} \div 1\frac{3}{4}$ _____

12. $5\frac{7}{8} \div 2\frac{1}{2}$ _____

Find each quotient.

13. $2\frac{1}{2} \div \frac{1}{4}$ _____

14. $100\frac{1}{8} \div 6\frac{1}{4}$ _____

15. $3\frac{2}{3} \div 1\frac{1}{2}$ _____

16. $6\frac{1}{8} \div 2\frac{2}{4}$ _____

17. $75\frac{1}{2} \div 5\frac{1}{2}$ _____

18. $1\frac{1}{6} \div 2\frac{2}{3}$ _____

19. $10\frac{2}{3} \div 4\frac{1}{3}$ _____

20. $18\frac{2}{9} \div 1\frac{1}{2}$ _____

21. $1\frac{1}{10} \div 1\frac{5}{6}$ _____

Practice 5-4

Dividing Mixed Numbers

Estimate each quotient.

1. $\frac{4}{5} \div \frac{7}{8}$

2. $2\frac{3}{7} \div \frac{5}{6}$

3. $12\frac{3}{8} \div 3\frac{3}{4}$

_____ _____ _____

4. $\frac{1}{8} \div \frac{11}{12}$

5. $17\frac{11}{13} \div 2\frac{7}{9}$

6. $51\frac{1}{5} \div 4\frac{9}{10}$

_____ _____ _____

7. $4 \div 1\frac{8}{11}$

8. $21\frac{2}{3} \div \frac{15}{17}$

9. $32\frac{5}{8} \div 2\frac{6}{11}$

_____ _____ _____

Find each quotient.

10. $1\frac{4}{5} \div \frac{1}{3}$

11. $1\frac{2}{3} \div \frac{1}{8}$

12. $3\frac{4}{7} \div 3\frac{1}{2}$

13. $3\frac{4}{5} \div 1\frac{5}{7}$

_____ _____ _____ _____

14. $\frac{2}{5} \div 4\frac{3}{5}$

15. $4\frac{1}{8} \div \frac{3}{7}$

16. $2\frac{4}{5} \div 4\frac{3}{4}$

17. $\frac{5}{6} \div 1\frac{3}{4}$

_____ _____ _____ _____

18. $1\frac{5}{7} \div 1\frac{2}{3}$

19. $\frac{1}{3} \div 2\frac{1}{6}$

20. $1\frac{4}{9} \div \frac{6}{7}$

21. $1\frac{3}{4} \div \frac{4}{5}$

_____ _____ _____ _____

22. $\frac{1}{2} \div 3\frac{1}{4}$

23. $4\frac{2}{7} \div 1\frac{1}{6}$

24. $\frac{4}{5} \div 3\frac{2}{5}$

25. $\frac{8}{9} \div 2\frac{5}{7}$

_____ _____ _____ _____

26. $\frac{1}{4} \div 1\frac{5}{9}$

27. $1\frac{3}{4} \div \frac{1}{5}$

28. $4\frac{2}{7} \div 1\frac{1}{2}$

29. $1\frac{1}{9} \div \frac{1}{5}$

_____ _____ _____ _____

30. $1\frac{1}{2} \div 1\frac{2}{3}$

31. $1\frac{5}{8} \div \frac{5}{9}$

32. $1\frac{3}{5} \div \frac{1}{3}$

33. $\frac{1}{2} \div 3\frac{5}{7}$

_____ _____ _____ _____

Anna bought a strip of fabric 10 yd long. She needs a $1\frac{1}{3}$-yd piece to make a pillow.

34. How many pillows can Anna make?

_____

35. Anna decides to make smaller pillows using $\frac{2}{3}$-yd pieces. How many small pillows can she make?

_____

36. A bulletin board is 56 in. wide and 36 in. high. How many $3\frac{1}{2}$-in. columns can be created?

_____

Reteaching 5-5

When solving multiplication equations, it may help to first find the numerator of the missing value and then the denominator. If the equation includes whole numbers or mixed numbers, you may need to rewrite these numbers as fractions.

Solve: $\frac{2}{5}x = \frac{4}{25}$.

① Think: What number times $\frac{2}{5}$ equals $\frac{4}{25}$? $\;\boxed{2 \times 2 = 4}$

② Then use mental math to find the numerator. $\frac{2}{5} \times \frac{?}{?} = \frac{4}{25}$

③ Use mental math to find the denominator. $\frac{2}{5} \times \frac{2}{?} = \frac{4}{25}$

$\boxed{5 \times 5 = 25}$

④ Check to see that the equation is true. $\frac{2}{5} \times \frac{2}{5} = \frac{4}{25}$ ✓

So, $x = \frac{2}{5}$.

Solve each equation. Check the solution.

1. $\frac{2}{3}x = \frac{8}{15}$

   $x =$ _____

2. $\frac{3}{4}x = \frac{9}{20}$

   $x =$ _____

3. $\frac{1}{3}x = 4$

   $x =$ _____

4. $\frac{3}{8}x = \frac{18}{16}$

   $x =$ _____

5. $\frac{3}{2}x = \frac{6}{10}$

   $x =$ _____

6. $\frac{9}{5}x = \frac{9}{25}$

   $x =$ _____

7. $\frac{8}{3}x = \frac{16}{27}$

   $x =$ _____

8. $\frac{5}{4}x = \frac{35}{48}$

   $x =$ _____

9. $\frac{9}{7}x = \frac{27}{35}$

   $x =$ _____

10. $\frac{10}{3}x = \frac{20}{27}$

    $x =$ _____

11. A wrestler weighed $112\frac{1}{2}$ pounds before the state meet. After the meet, the wrestler weighed $\frac{49}{50}$ of his original weight. How much did the wrestler weigh after the meet?

12. A number divided by 4 equals $10\frac{1}{8}$. What is the number?

_____

Practice 5-5

Solving Fraction Equations by Multiplying

Solve each equation. Check the solution.

1. $\frac{3}{13}n = \frac{1}{2}$

   $n =$ _____

2. $\frac{6}{7}f = \frac{1}{3}$

   $f =$ _____

3. $\frac{7}{19}f = \frac{1}{2}$

   $f =$ _____

4. $\frac{5}{18}n = 2$

   $n =$ _____

5. $\frac{5}{8}n = 1$

   $n =$ _____

6. $\frac{1}{2}u = \frac{3}{5}$

   $u =$ _____

7. $\frac{3}{7}q = \frac{3}{8}$

   $q =$ _____

8. $\frac{5}{14}c = \frac{1}{2}$

   $c =$ _____

9. $\frac{3}{2}b = \frac{6}{7}$

   $b =$ _____

10. $\frac{1}{4}n = 2$

    $n =$ _____

11. $\frac{7}{8}t = 3$

    $t =$ _____

12. $\frac{5}{12}h = \frac{3}{5}$

    $h =$ _____

13. $\frac{4}{9}v = \frac{1}{4}$

    $v =$ _____

14. $\frac{8}{25}h = 2$

    $h =$ _____

15. $\frac{10}{7}h = \frac{1}{2}$

    $h =$ _____

16. $\frac{2}{3}w = 3$

    $w =$ _____

17. $\frac{8}{17}d = \frac{1}{3}$

    $d =$ _____

18. $\frac{3}{2}v = \frac{1}{2}$

    $v =$ _____

19. $\frac{7}{3}z = 1$

    $z =$ _____

20. $\frac{5}{9}z = \frac{1}{3}$

    $z =$ _____

21. $\frac{10}{17}m = 4$

    $m =$ _____

Solve.

22. The largest U.S. standard postage stamp ever issued has a width of about 1 inch, which was $\frac{3}{4}$ of the height of the stamp. Write and solve an equation to find the height of the stamp.

    _____

23. Candace said, "I'm thinking of a fraction. If I divide it by $\frac{1}{2}$, I get $\frac{3}{11}$." What fraction was Candace thinking of?

    _____

Reteaching 5-6

A mystery game has 3 rooms. Each room has 3 desks. Each desk has 3 drawers, and each drawer has 3 dollars. If you are able to collect all the money, how many dollars would this be?

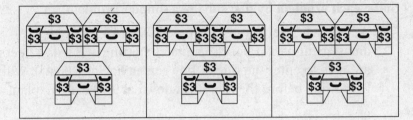

Read and Understand   What is the object of the game?
The object is to collect all the money.
What does the problem ask you to find?
Find how much money is hidden in all 3 rooms.

Plan and Solve   If you cannot solve the entire problem at once, how can you break it down into simpler problems?
Find the amount of money in one room.
Then multiply by 3.

For one room multiply:
3 (desks) × 3 (drawers) × 3 (dollars).
There is $27 in one room. 3 × $27 = $81. There is $81 in all three rooms.

Look Back and Check   How does solving a simpler problem help find the solution to the original problem?
The strategy allows you to work with easier numbers.

Solve each problem by first solving a simpler problem.

1. Another game has 7 rooms, each with 7 paintings. Behind each painting are 7 safes. Inside each safe are 7 security boxes, each with $70. How much money is hidden in the house?

2. If someone enters one of the 7 rooms while you are there collecting the money, you must give that person the contents of one safe. Suppose this happens to you in all 7 rooms. How much would you have at the end of the game?

3. Six students are playing a game. Each student plays the game once with each of the other students. How many games are played?

4. Twelve students each have 2 bookbags. Each bookbag contains 4 books. Each book costs $10.95. How much do the books cost altogether?

Practice 5-6

Solve each problem by first solving a simpler problem.

1. At 8:00 P.M., there are 243 people in line for a ride at an amusement park. Every 12 minutes starting at 8 P.M., 42 people are able to enter the ride. A boy gets in line at 8:00 P.M. Will he get to ride before the ride shuts down at 9:00 P.M.? Explain.

2. The astronauts who landed on the moon brought back about 842 pounds of moon rocks. Dividing the cost of these moon flights by the weight of the rocks, it is estimated that the rocks cost $3,000,000 per ounce. What was the approximate cost of these moon flights?

3. While an adult is asleep, his or her heart can pump about 80 gal of blood per hour. About how many gallons of blood will the heart pump during a week of sleep if an adult sleeps 7 h each night?

Choose a strategy to solve each problem.

4. The Language Club includes students who are enrolled in Latin, German, Spanish, or French. Each person, including John, is enrolled in only one foreign language. Christine does not speak French. Judy is enrolled in German or Latin. Pepe is enrolled in Latin or Spanish. Christine and the person taking Spanish often walk to school together. Christine and the person who is taking German are best friends. Who is enrolled in which course?

5. What is the sum of all odd numbers from 101 to 200?

6. A small hummingbird beats its wings 70 times per second. How many times will it beat its wings in 8 h?

7. It takes the sound of thunder five seconds to travel one mile. How far away is the thunder if it takes 45 s to reach you?

8. A company with 628 employees is taking all the employees to see a baseball game. The company will hire buses. If each bus holds 34 passengers, will 15 buses be enough?

Reteaching 5-7

Choose an appropriate customary unit of measure to describe the following:

length of a train engine You need a unit to measure length. A train engine will be quite long, so choose feet or yards.	weight of a train engine You need a unit to measure weight. Since a train engine will be quite heavy, choose tons.
amount of liquid in a large bucket You need a unit to measure capacity. A bucket is likely to contain quite a bit of water, so choose quarts or gallons.	length of a CD case You need a unit to measure length. A CD case is quite small, so choose inches.
weight of a bale of straw You need a unit to measure weight. A bale of straw is heavy, so choose pounds.	amount of liquid in a bottle of eye drops You need a unit to measure capacity. A bottle of eye drops will be very small, so choose fluid ounces.

Choose an appropriate unit for each measurement. Explain.

1. the length of a garden

_____

_____

2. the length of a hummingbird

_____

_____

Choose an appropriate unit for each weight. Explain.

3. the weight of a letter

_____

4. the weight of steel girders

_____

Choose an appropriate unit for each capacity. Explain.

5. a pitcher of juice

_____

_____

6. the water in an aquarium

_____

_____

Compare using <, ≈, or >.

7. weight of a tank [ ] 100 pounds

8. length of a TV remote [ ] 5 inches

Practice 5-7

Use the table to choose an appropriate unit of measurement for each item. Explain.

Customary Units of Measure

	Name	Approximate Comparison
Length	inch	Length of a soda bottle cap
	foot	Length of an adult male's foot
	mile	Length of 14 football fields
Weight	ounce	Weight of a slice of bread
	pound	Weight of a loaf of bread
	ton	Weight of two grand pianos
Capacity	cup	Amount of water in a drinking glass
	quart	Amount in a bottle of fruit punch
	gallon	Amount in a large can of paint

1. height of a stop sign

_____

_____

2. length of a leaf

_____

_____

3. width of a door

_____

_____

4. depth of the ocean

_____

_____

5. weight of a small notebook

_____

_____

6. weight of a couch

_____

_____

7. weight of a garbage truck

_____

_____

8. weight of a box of books

_____

_____

9. water in a swimming pool

_____

_____

10. water in a bathtub

_____

_____

11. a soup in a can

_____

_____

12. milk in a carton

_____

_____

Compare using <, =, or >.

13. water you use to wash dishes ☐ 1 cup

14. the depth of the Grand Canyon ☐ 30 miles

15. the weight of a cereal bowl ☐ 6 ounces

Course 1 Chapter 5

Reteaching 5-8

Complete the statement: $5\frac{5}{8}$ c = __?__ fl oz

(1) Find the relationship between cups and fluid ounces: 1 c = 8 fl oz

(2) Since there are 8 fluid ounces in each cup, multiply the number of cups by 8.

$$5\frac{5}{8} \times 8 = \frac{45}{8} \times 8$$

$$= \frac{45}{1\,\cancel{8}} \times \frac{\cancel{8}^{1}}{1}$$

$$= 45$$

$5\frac{5}{8}$ c = 45 fl oz

Subtract: 9 ft 8 in. − 2 ft 11 in.

(1) Find the relationship between feet and inches: 1 ft = 12 in.

(2) Use the relationship to rename 9 feet 8 inches as 8 feet 20 inches.

(3) Subtract.

$$
\begin{array}{rcr}
9\ \text{ft}\ \ 8\ \text{in.} & \rightarrow & 8\ \text{ft}\ 20\ \text{in.}\\
-\ 2\ \text{ft}\ 11\ \text{in.} & & -\ 2\ \text{ft}\ 11\ \text{in.}\\
\hline
& & 6\ \text{ft}\ \ 9\ \text{in.}
\end{array}
$$

9 ft 8 in. − 2 ft 11 in. = 6 ft 9 in.

To compare amounts, first change them to the same unit.

Compare: 25 fl oz __?__ 3 c → 25 fl oz __?__ 24 fl oz

25 fl oz   >   24 fl oz

25 fl oz   >   3 c

Complete each statement.

1. 12 ft = __?__ yd _____

2. 32 qt = __?__ gal _____

3. $1\frac{1}{2}$ mi = __?__ ft _____

4. 15 pt = __?__ qt _____

5. 440 yd = __?__ mi _____

6. $2\frac{1}{2}$ T = __?__ lb _____

7. $9\frac{1}{4}$ c = __?__ fl oz _____

8. 40 oz = __?__ lb _____

9. $8\frac{1}{4}$ ft = __?__ in. _____

Add or subtract.

10. $\begin{array}{r} 3\ \text{pt}\ 1\ \text{c} \\ +\ 4\ \text{pt}\ 1\ \text{c} \\ \hline \end{array}$

11. $\begin{array}{r} 4\ \text{yd}\ 1\ \text{ft} \\ -\ 1\ \text{yd}\ 2\ \text{ft} \\ \hline \end{array}$

12. $\begin{array}{r} 5\ \text{lb}\ 20\ \text{oz} \\ +\ 8\ \text{lb}\ 12\ \text{oz} \\ \hline \end{array}$

_____   _____   _____

Use <, =, or > to complete each statement.

13. 43 in. ☐ 4 ft

14. $8\frac{1}{2}$ gal ☐ 136 c

15. 108 in. ☐ $3\frac{1}{2}$ yd

16. $2\frac{1}{2}$ lb ☐ 40 oz

17. 7,000 lb ☐ $3\frac{1}{4}$ t

18. $5\frac{1}{2}$ pt ☐ 3 qt

19. A semi-truck can hold 8,500 pounds of cargo. How many tons can it hold?

_____

Practice 5-8

Changing Units in the Customary System

Complete each statement.

1. $7\frac{1}{2}$ ft = _____ yd

2. 45 in. = _____ ft

3. $1\frac{1}{4}$ mi = _____ ft

4. $2\frac{1}{2}$ lb = _____ oz

5. 28 fl oz = _____ c

6. $2\frac{3}{4}$ T = _____ lb

7. 3 lb = _____ oz

8. 10 pt = _____ qt

Add or subtract.

9.   8 ft 3 in.
  − 3 ft 5 in.

10.   12 qt 1 pt
  + 11 qt 1 pt

11.   9 yd 15 in.
  + 7 yd 28 in.

12.   105 lb 8 oz
  − 98 lb 12 oz

13.   3 c 7 fl oz
  + 4 c 6 fl oz

14.   13 yd 2 ft
  − 6 yd 1 ft

Solve.

15. The odometer of an automobile shows tenths of a mile.
How many feet are in $\frac{1}{10}$ mi?

_____

16. How many inches are in one mile?

_____

17. Jarel bought 3 containers of cottage cheese, each weighing 24 oz.
How many pounds did she buy?

_____

18. Katie poured 12 oz of juice from a full 6-qt container. How many
cups were left in the container?

_____

19. The food committee for the end-of-the-year class picnic plans to
serve 4-oz hamburger patties. How many pounds of meat should
be purchased to make 125 hamburgers?

_____

Use <, =, or > to complete each statement.

20. $4\frac{1}{3}$ ft ☐ 50 in.

21. 136 oz ☐ $8\frac{1}{2}$ lb

22. 26 fl oz ☐ 3 c

23. 5 qt ☐ $1\frac{1}{4}$ gal

24. 8 yd ☐ 21 ft

25. 4,500 lb ☐ $3\frac{1}{2}$ T

Reteaching 6-1

A *ratio* is a comparison of two numbers by division. Each number in a ratio is called a *term*. You can write a ratio in three different ways. For example, the ratio 4 to 5 can be written:

4 to 5

4 : 5

$\frac{4}{5}$

Equal ratios name the same number. They have the same *simplest form*.

- To find equal ratios, multiply *or* divide both the numerator and denominator of a ratio by the same number.

Find a ratio equal to $\frac{4}{7}$.

$$\frac{4}{7} = \frac{4 \times 2}{7 \times 2} = \frac{8}{14}$$

$\frac{8}{14}$ is equal to $\frac{4}{7}$.

Find the simplest form for the ratio $\frac{16}{20}$.

$$\frac{16}{20} = \frac{16 \div 4}{20 \div 4} = \frac{4}{5}$$

$\frac{4}{5}$ is the simplest form for $\frac{16}{20}$.

Write three different ratios equal to each ratio.

1. $\frac{2}{5}$

2. 1 : 3

3. 3 to 4

4. 5 : 8

5. 2 to 7

6. $\frac{1}{5}$

7. 12 to 20

8. 6 : 16

Write each ratio in simplest form.

9. 32 : 16

10. $\frac{14}{24}$

11. $\frac{36}{50}$

12. 60 : 25

13. $\frac{25}{40}$

14. 60 : 180

15. $\frac{75}{120}$

16. 80 : 20

Find the value that makes the ratios equal.

17. 3 : 4, _?_ : 16

18. 20 to 25, 40 to _?_

19. 9 to 12, 81 to _?_

20. 7 : 10, _?_ : 100

21. 1 to 8, _?_ to 24

22. 30 : 120, 90 : _?_

23. 5 : 100, 25 : _?_

24. $\frac{7}{56}, \frac{?}{280}$

25. $\frac{6}{12}, \frac{36}{?}$

Practice 6-1

Ratios

Write a ratio in three ways to compare each.

1. saws to pliers

_____

2. hammers to nails

_____

3. saws to nails

_____

4. nails to saws

_____

5. hammers to pliers

_____

6. pliers to saws

_____

7. pliers to nails

_____

8. saws to hammers

_____

9. nails to hammers

_____

Write each ratio as a fraction in simplest form..

10. pencils : squares

_____

11. flowers : pencils

_____

12. pencils : flowers

_____

13. pencils : circles

_____

14. squares : flowers

_____

15. flowers : squares

_____

16. squares : pencils

_____

17. circles : flowers

_____

Find the value that makes the ratios equal.

18. 4 to 10, 2 to _?_

_____

19. 8 : 3, _?_ : 9

_____

20. 51 to 18, _?_ to 6

_____

21. $\frac{12}{12}$, $\frac{?}{20}$

_____

22. 98 : 46, 49 : _?_

_____

23. $\frac{15}{7}$, $\frac{?}{21}$

_____

24. 1 : 1, 8 : _?_

_____

25. $\frac{28}{56}$, $\frac{?}{14}$

_____

26. 36 to 12, _?_ to 1

_____

Reteaching 6-2

A *rate* is a ratio that compares quantities that are measured in different units. Suppose a sprinter runs 100 yards in 10 seconds.

$\dfrac{100 \text{ yd}}{10 \text{ s}}$ compares yards to seconds.

A *unit rate* compares a quantity to one unit of another quantity.

You can find the unit rate by dividing by the denominator.

$$\dfrac{100 \text{ yd} \div 10}{10 \text{ s} \div 10} = \dfrac{10 \text{ yd}}{1 \text{ s}}$$

10 yards per second is the sprinter's unit rate.

Find the unit rate for each situation.

1. $70 for 10 shirts

2. $150 for 3 games

3. $20 for 5 toys

_____

_____

_____

4. $120 for 6 shirts

5. $45 for 5 boxes

6. $132 for 3 books

_____

_____

_____

7. $100 for 5 rackets

8. $56 for 7 hours

9. $1.98 for 6 cans

_____

_____

_____

Write the unit rate as a ratio. Then find an equal ratio.

10. The cost is $4.25 for 1 item. Find the cost of 5 items.

11. There are 7 cheerleaders in a squad. Find the number of cheerleaders on 12 squads.

12. The cost is $10.10 for 1 item. Find the cost of 10 items.

13. There are 2.54 centimeters per one inch. Find the number of centimeters in 5 inches.

14. The cost is $8.50 for 1 item. Find the cost of 3 items.

For Exercises 15–18, tell which unit rate is greater.

15. Dillan scores 24 points in 2 games. Eric scores 40 points in 4 games.

16. A fern grows 4 inches in 2 months. A tree grows 6 inches in 4 months.

17. Tyler jogs 4 miles in 32 minutes. Joey jogs 2 miles in 18 minutes.

18. Dixie drinks 2 cups of water in 5 minutes. Dale drinks 10 cups of water in 12 minutes.

Practice 6-2

Find the unit rate for each situation.

1. 44 breaths in 2 minutes

   _____

2. 72 players on 9 teams

   _____

3. 60 miles in 2 hours

   _____

4. 15 pages in 30 minutes

   _____

5. 48 questions in 4 quizzes

   _____

6. $3 for 4 packages

   _____

Write the unit rate as a ratio. Then find an equal ratio.

7. There are 12 inches in a foot. Find the number of inches in 6 feet.

   _____

8. The cost is $8.50 for 1 shirt. Find the cost of 4 shirts.

   _____

9. There are 365 days in a year. Find the number of days in 3 years.

   _____

10. There are 6 cans per box. Find the number of cans in 11 boxes.

   _____

11. There are 5 students in a group. Find the number of students in
    5 groups.

   _____

12. There are 70 pages in a notebook. Find the number of pages in
    8 notebooks.

   _____

Find each unit price.

13. $5 for 10 pounds _____

14. 40 ounces for $12 _____

15. $6 for 10 pens _____

16. $60 for 5 books _____

17. $22 for 3 shirts _____

18. $35 for 25 tapes _____

Reteaching 6-3

A *proportion* is an equation stating that two ratios are equal.

Does $\frac{4}{10} = \frac{6}{15}$?

First, simplify each fraction.

$\frac{4}{10} = \frac{2}{5}$, and $\frac{6}{15} = \frac{2}{5}$

So, $\frac{4}{10} = \frac{6}{15}$.

You can use mental math to solve proportions.

Use mental math to solve $\frac{3}{5} = \frac{15}{?}$.

$3 \times 5 = 15$, so $5 \times 5 = 25$

So, $\frac{3}{5} = \frac{15}{25}$.

Do the ratios in each pair form a proportion?

1. $\frac{25}{100}, \frac{4}{16}$

2. $\frac{15}{20}, \frac{4}{5}$

3. $\frac{35}{40}, \frac{45}{50}$

4. $\frac{54}{9}, \frac{36}{6}$

5. $\frac{7}{11}, \frac{49}{77}$

6. $\frac{18}{24}, \frac{24}{30}$

7. $\frac{3}{5}, \frac{5}{3}$

8. $\frac{9}{10}, \frac{19}{20}$

9. $\frac{8}{24}, \frac{1}{3}$

Find the value that completes each proportion.

10. $\frac{6}{10} = \frac{3}{?}$

11. $\frac{8}{16} = \frac{4}{?}$

12. $\frac{9}{21} = \frac{?}{7}$

13. $\frac{2}{?} = \frac{10}{50}$

14. $\frac{11}{?} = \frac{33}{15}$

15. $\frac{?}{25} = \frac{14}{50}$

16. $\frac{6}{30} = \frac{?}{90}$

17. $\frac{45}{9} = \frac{25}{?}$

18. $\frac{18}{?} = \frac{2}{9}$

19. A basketball player bounces the ball one time for every three steps. How many times will the player bounce the ball for twelve steps?

_____

20. Four laps around the track equals one mile. How many miles does sixteen laps equal?

_____

Practice 6-3

Understanding Proportions

Do the ratios in each pair form a proportion?

1. $\frac{8}{9}, \frac{4}{3}$

   _____

2. $\frac{20}{16}, \frac{18}{15}$

   _____

3. $\frac{18}{12}, \frac{21}{14}$

   _____

4. $\frac{21}{27}, \frac{35}{45}$

   _____

5. $\frac{18}{22}, \frac{45}{55}$

   _____

6. $\frac{38}{52}, \frac{57}{80}$

   _____

7. $\frac{10}{65}, \frac{18}{87}$

   _____

8. $\frac{51}{48}, \frac{68}{64}$

   _____

Find the value that completes each proportion.

9. $\frac{4}{5} = \frac{?}{15}$

   _____

10. $\frac{8}{?} = \frac{4}{15}$

    _____

11. $\frac{3}{2} = \frac{21}{?}$

    _____

12. $\frac{?}{5} = \frac{32}{20}$

    _____

13. $\frac{7}{8} = \frac{?}{32}$

    _____

14. $\frac{5}{4} = \frac{15}{?}$

    _____

15. 8 to 12 = __?__ to 6

    _____

16. 9 : 12 = 3 : __?__

    _____

17. In 1910, there were about 220 families for every 1,000 people in the United States. If a certain town had a population of 56,000, about how many families would you expect to find in the town?

    _____

18. For every 100 families with TV sets, about 12 families like watching sports. In a town of 23,400 families who all have TV sets, how many families would you expect to like watching sports?

    _____

19. In 1800, there were only about 6 people per square mile of land in the U.S. What was the approximate population in 1800 if there were about 364,700 square miles in the U.S.?

    _____

Reteaching 6-4

If two ratios are equal, they form a *proportion*.

$$\frac{1}{5} = \frac{2}{10}$$

Equal ratios have equal cross products.

$\frac{1}{5} \diagup\!\!\!\!\diagdown \frac{2}{10}$ ---→ $5 \times 2 = 10$
---→ $1 \times 10 = 10$

Equal cross products also show that a proportion is true.

$\frac{1}{6} \diagup\!\!\!\!\diagdown \frac{3}{18}$ ---→ $6 \times 3 = 18$
---→ $1 \times 18 = 18$

The cross products are equal, so the ratios are equal and form a proportion.

You can find the missing term in a proportion by using *cross products*.

Solve $\frac{4}{7} = \frac{12}{n}$.

① Write the cross products. $4 \times n = 7 \times 12$

② Simplify. $4n = 84$

③ Divide by 4. $\frac{4n}{4} = \frac{84}{4}$

④ Simplify. $n = 21$

Does each pair of ratios form a proportion?

1. $\frac{4}{7}, \frac{8}{14}$

2. $\frac{5}{2}, \frac{10}{4}$

3. $\frac{6}{8}, \frac{3}{5}$

4. $\frac{15}{3}, \frac{10}{2}$

_____

5. $\frac{15}{45}, \frac{25}{60}$

6. $\frac{12}{16}, \frac{15}{20}$

7. $\frac{9}{10}, \frac{19}{20}$

8. $\frac{32}{12}, \frac{8}{3}$

_____

9. $\frac{56}{8}, \frac{1}{7}$

10. $\frac{4}{7}, \frac{14}{21}$

11. $\frac{40}{50}, \frac{8}{10}$

12. $\frac{5}{15}, \frac{9}{27}$

_____

Solve each proportion.

13. $\frac{n}{5} = \frac{2}{10}$

14. $\frac{9}{n} = \frac{27}{3}$

15. $\frac{30}{6} = \frac{a}{9}$

16. $\frac{42}{12} = \frac{x}{4}$

_____

17. $\frac{t}{24} = \frac{3}{8}$

18. $\frac{16}{12} = \frac{r}{18}$

19. $\frac{18}{32} = \frac{27}{m}$

20. $\frac{48}{30} = \frac{32}{e}$

_____

21. $\frac{5}{6} = \frac{h}{36}$

22. $\frac{60}{24} = \frac{w}{12}$

23. $\frac{11}{14} = \frac{33}{y}$

24. $\frac{90}{25} = \frac{x}{5}$

_____

25. $\frac{10}{5} = \frac{6}{t}$

26. $\frac{9}{a} = \frac{3}{5}$

27. $\frac{b}{2} = \frac{16}{4}$

28. $\frac{12}{16} = \frac{n}{4}$

_____

Practice 6-4 **Using Cross Products**

Does each pair of ratios form a proportion?

1. $\frac{14}{21}, \frac{8}{12}$ _____

2. $\frac{12}{18}, \frac{16}{24}$ _____

3. $\frac{24}{25}, \frac{12}{15}$ _____

4. $\frac{28}{42}, \frac{26}{39}$ _____

5. $\frac{16}{24}, \frac{19}{27}$ _____

6. $\frac{50}{8}, \frac{155}{25}$ _____

7. $\frac{9}{10}, \frac{40.5}{45}$ _____

8. $\frac{85}{90}, \frac{45}{50}$ _____

Solve each proportion.

9. $\frac{9}{7} = \frac{27}{x}$

_____

10. $\frac{17}{12} = \frac{34}{y}$

_____

11. $\frac{6}{a} = \frac{36}{54}$

12. $\frac{m}{25} = \frac{9}{75}$

13. $\frac{31}{c} = \frac{93}{15}$

14. $\frac{14}{35} = \frac{m}{5}$

15. $\frac{12}{27} = \frac{4}{w}$

16. $\frac{46}{52} = \frac{23}{y}$

Write and solve a proportion for each problem.

17. It costs $15 to buy 5 packs of baseball cards. How much will it cost to buy 25 packs of baseball cards?

_____

18. There are 35 children and 6 adults at a preschool. To keep the same child to adult ratio, how many adults are needed for 140 children?

_____

19. Sam is making dinner for four people. The recipe calls for 15 ounces of steak. How much steak will he need if he makes dinner for 10 people?

_____

20. Brenda is selling magazines. Two subscriptions sell for $15.99. How much will 8 subscriptions cost?

_____

21. A baseball player made 14 errors in 156 games this year. About how many errors would you expect the player to make in 350 games?

_____

Reteaching 6-5

The *scale drawing* at the right shows a game field at Weld Middle School. The *scale* is a ratio that compares length on a drawing to the actual length. Here, every inch equals 36 yards on the actual field.

You can write the scale as a ratio in fraction form:

$$\frac{\text{drawing (in.)}}{\text{actual (yd)}} = \frac{1}{36}$$

To find the actual length of the field:

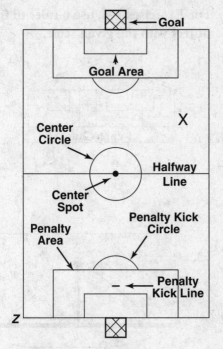

scale: 1 in. : 36 yd

(1) Measure the scale drawing.   3 in.

(2) Write the scale as a ratio. $\frac{1}{36}$

(3) Use the scale ratio in a proportion. $\frac{1}{36} = \frac{3}{n}$

(4) Write cross products. $1 \times n = 3 \times 36$

(5) Solve for *n*. $n = 108$

The actual length is 108 yards.

Use the scale drawing above to find the actual size.

1. Find the width of the field.

   _____

2. Find the perimeter of the field.

   _____

3. Find the measure of the shorter side of the penalty area.

   _____

4. Find the distance from the center spot to the front of the goal.

   _____

5. Brian kicks the ball from the penalty kick line to the opposite goal area. About how far does he kick the ball?

   _____

6. Kaitlin makes a direct kick from the spot marked X. She scores by getting the ball into the goal nearest her. About how far does she kick the ball?

   _____

Write each scale as a ratio.

7. a 12-inch model of a 60-foot boat

   _____

8. a 6-inch drawing of an 18-inch TV

   _____

9. a 4-centimeter model of a 28-centimeter hammer

   _____

10. a 9-inch drawing of a 54-foot garden

   _____

Practice 6-5

For Exercises 1–6, use a ruler to find the dimensions of the actual object with the given scale.

1.

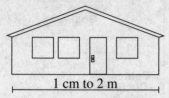

1 cm to 2 m

_____

2.

1 in. to 15 ft

_____

3.

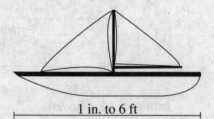

1 in. to 6 ft

_____

4.

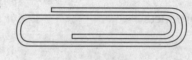

1 cm to 5 mm

_____

5.

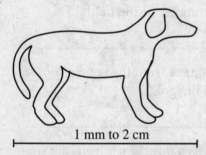

1 mm to 2 cm

_____

6.

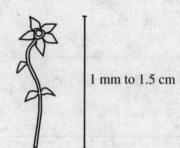

1 mm to 1.5 cm

_____

7. Find the measure in centimeters of your thumb from the tip of your fingernail to where it meets your wrist. If you drew a $\frac{3}{4}$-size picture of yourself, how long would your thumb be in the drawing?

_____

8. The length of a wall in a floor plan is $6\frac{1}{2}$ inches The actual wall is 78 feet long. Find the scale of the floor plan.

_____

9. The height of a building is $3\frac{3}{8}$ inches on a scale drawing. Find the actual height of the building if the scale used is 1 inch : 4 feet.

_____

Reteaching 6-6

- To *write a percent as a fraction* in simplest form, first write a fraction with a denominator of 100. Then simplify.

    $74\% = \frac{74}{100} = \frac{37}{50}$

- To *write a percent as a decimal*, first write a fraction with a denominator of 100. Then write the decimal.

    $74\% = \frac{74}{100} = 0.74$

- To *write a decimal as a percent*, move the decimal point two places to the right.

    $0.23 = 23\%$

Here are two ways to *write a fraction as a percent*.

- Write an equivalent fraction with a denominator of 100, then write the percent.

    $\frac{3}{20} = \frac{15}{100} = 15\%$

- Divide the numerator by the denominator.

$$\frac{3}{8} = \begin{array}{r} 0.375 \\ 8\overline{)3.000} \\ -2\,4 \\ \hline 60 \\ -56 \\ \hline 40 \\ -40 \\ \hline 0 \end{array} = 37.5\%$$

$\uparrow$ Move the decimal point two places to the right.

So, $\frac{3}{8} = 37.5\%$.

Write each percent as a decimal and as a fraction in simplest form.

1. 30%

2. 14%

3. 16%

4. 5%

5. 92%

6. 80%

7. 21%

8. 38%

Write each fraction or decimal as a percent.

9. $\frac{17}{25}$

10. 0.85

11. 0.16

12. $\frac{5}{40}$

13. $\frac{7}{200}$

14. $\frac{1}{10}$

15. 0.64

16. 0.008

17. $\frac{9}{20}$

18. $\frac{6}{15}$

19. 0.32

20. 0.07

21. $\frac{13}{100}$

22. $\frac{45}{50}$

23. 0.010

24. 0.60

Practice 6-6

Percents, Fractions, and Decimals

Write each percent as a decimal and as a fraction in simplest form.

1. 46% _____   **2.** 17% _____   **3.** 90% _____   **4.** 5% _____

Write each decimal as a percent and as a fraction in simplest form.

5. 0.02 _____   **6.** 0.45 _____   **7.** 0.4 _____   **8.** 0.92 _____

Write each fraction as a decimal and as a percent.

9. $\frac{3}{5}$ _____   **10.** $\frac{7}{10}$ _____   **11.** $\frac{13}{25}$ _____   **12.** $\frac{17}{20}$ _____

The table shows the fraction of students who participated in extracurricular activities from 1965 to 2000. Complete the table by writing each fraction as a percent.

Students' Extracurricular Choices

Year	1965	1970	1975	1980	1985	1990	1995	2000
Student participation (fraction)	$\frac{3}{4}$	$\frac{8}{10}$	$\frac{17}{20}$	$\frac{39}{50}$	$\frac{21}{25}$	$\frac{19}{25}$	$\frac{87}{100}$	$\frac{9}{10}$
Student participation (percent)								

Write each fraction or decimal as a percent. Write the percent (without the percent sign) in the puzzle.

ACROSS

1. $\frac{3}{5}$

2. $\frac{1}{5}$

3. 0.55

5. 0.23

6. $\frac{7}{20}$

7. 0.17

9. 0.4

10. $\frac{9}{25}$

DOWN

1. $\frac{13}{20}$

2. 0.25

3. $\frac{1}{2}$

4. $\frac{3}{20}$

5. 0.24

6. $\frac{3}{10}$

7. 0.1

8. $\frac{4}{25}$

Reteaching 6-7

Finding a Percent of a Number

You can find 70% of 90 using different methods.

Use mental math.

① Write the percent as a fraction in simplest form.

$$70\% = \frac{70}{100} = \frac{7}{10}$$

② Multiply by the fraction.

$$\frac{7}{10} \times \frac{90}{1} = \frac{630}{10} = 63$$

70% of 90 = 63.

Use a proportion.

① Write a proportion.

$$\frac{70}{100} = \frac{c}{90}$$

② Write cross products and simplify.

$$100 \times c = 70 \times 90$$
$$100c = 6{,}300$$

③ Solve.

$$c = \frac{6{,}300}{100}$$
$$c = 63$$

70% of 90 = 63.

Find each answer using mental math.

1. 45% of 60

2. 60% of 160

3. 15% of 220

4. 90% of 80

5. 35% of 60

6. 70% of 350

Find each answer using a proportion.

7. 40% of 60

8. 85% of 300

9. 15% of 160

10. 22% of 500

11. 37% of 400

12. 68% of 250

Find each answer.

13. 25% of 100

14. 70% of 70

15. 10% of 70

16. 75% of 40

17. 80% of 50

18. 12% of 60

19. 24% of 80

20. 45% of 90

21. 60% of 72

22. 55% of 120

23. 95% of 180

24. 16% of 80

Practice 6-7

Find each answer.

1. 15% of 20   **2.** 40% of 80   **3.** 20% of 45   **4.** 18% of 70

_____   _____   _____   _____

5. 90% of 120   **6.** 65% of 700   **7.** 25% of 84   **8.** 63% of 80

_____   _____   _____   _____

9. 60% of 50   **10.** 45% of 90   **11.** 12% of 94   **12.** 15% of 52

_____   _____   _____   _____

13. 37% of 80   **14.** 25% of 16   **15.** 63% of 800   **16.** 72% of 950

_____   _____   _____   _____

17. 55% of 250   **18.** 18% of 420   **19.** 33% of 140   **20.** 53% of 400

_____   _____   _____   _____

Solve each problem.

21. Teri used 60% of 20 gallons of paint. How much did she use? _____

22. The Badgers won 75% of their 32 games this year. How many games did they win? _____

23. Vivian earned $540 last month. She saved 30% of this money. How much did she save? _____

24. A survey of the students at Lakeside School yielded the results shown below. There are 1,400 students enrolled at Lakeside. Complete the table for the number of students in each activity.

How Lakeside Students Spend Their Time on Saturday

Activity	Percent of Students	Number of Students
Baby-sitting	22%	
Sports	26%	
Job	15%	
At home	10%	
Tutoring	10%	
Other	17%	

Reteaching 6-8

You can estimate a percent of a number using mental math.

Example: Estimate 19% of $83.

① Round to convenient numbers.

20% of 80

② Find 10% of 80.

10% of 80 = 8.

③ 20% of 80 is 2 times as much.

20% of 80 is 2×8, or 16.

19% of 83 is about 16.

Estimate each amount.

1. 50% of 41	**2.** 20% of 99	**3.** 10% of 73
4. 40% of 59	**5.** 1% of 94	**6.** 5% of 313
7. 70% of 498	**8.** 15% of 172	**9.** 25% of 154
10. 90% of 81	**11.** 30% of 60	**12.** 15% of 401
13. 40% of 23	**14.** 20% of 178	**15.** 75% of 21
16. 25% of 216	**17.** 50% of 77	**18.** 15% of 39
19. 3% of 887	**20.** 70% of 419	**21.** 80% of 69

22. A baseball glove is on sale for 75% off the original price of $96.25. Estimate the sale price of the glove.

_____

Practice 6-8

Estimate each amount.

1. 81% of 60

_____

2. 20% of 490

_____

3. 48% of 97

_____

4. 72% of 80

_____

5. 18% of 90

_____

6. 21% of 80

_____

7. 39% of 200

_____

8. 81% of 150

_____

9. 68% of 250

_____

10. 73% of 99

_____

Solve each problem.

11. Mr. Andropolis wants to leave the waitress a 12% tip. Estimate the tip he should leave if the family's bill is $32.46.

_____

12. Michael receives a 9.8% raise. He currently earns $1,789.46 per month. Estimate the amount by which his monthly earnings will increase.

_____

13. Estimate the sales tax and final cost of a book that costs $12.95 with a sales tax of 6%.

_____

14. A real estate agent receives a 9% commission for every house sold. Suppose she sold a house for $112,000. Estimate her commission.

_____

15. A jacket costs $94.95. It is on sale for 30% off. Estimate the sale price.

_____

Reteaching 6-9

You can organize information needed to solve a problem by *writing an equation*. Equations are useful when modeling a situation.

Example: Franklin has $25. He needs to buy diapers for $12.99. He wants to buy as much baby formula as he can. Each jar of formula costs $.79. How many jars of formula can he buy?

First, you know Frank must buy diapers for $12.99, and he has $25. You need to find out how much money he has left to spend on formula.

Frank has $25 − $12.99, or $12.01. You can write an equation to solve the problem.

Let j = the number of jars of formula Frank can buy.

$0.79 \times j = 12.01$ Then, solve for j.

$$j = \frac{12.01}{0.79}$$

$$j = 15.20$$

Since jars are sold in whole containers, Frank can buy 15 jars of formula.

Solve each problem by writing an equation.

1. A printer is on sale for $129.99. This is 25% off the regular price. What is the regular price of the printer?

   _____

2. Janie sold 250 magazine subscriptions for school this year. The number is down 12% from last year. How many subscriptions did Janie sell last year?

   _____

3. Barbara needs to buy a math book and some paper. She has $50. The math book costs $35, and paper costs $3.50 per package. How many packages of paper can Barbara buy?

   _____

4. Ice skates on sale for 25% off cost $45. What is the regular price of the skates?

   _____

5. Your homemade chili has 12 fewer fat grams than your favorite restaurant's chili. This is 10% less fat than the restaurant's chili. How many fat grams does the restaurant's chili have?

   _____

Practice 6-9

Problem Solving: Write an Equation

Solve each problem by writing an equation.

1. Bethany buys five dolls. She gives the store clerk $50 and receives $16 in change. Each doll costs the same amount. How much does each doll cost?

_____

_____

2. A restaurant offers a 13% discount on chicken wings on Mondays. If Travis eats $7.95 worth of chicken wings on Friday, how much would those wings cost on Monday?

_____

_____

3. Last year, the Widget Corporation had $650,000 in sales. This year, sales are down 4%. How much did the Widget Corporation sell this year?

_____

_____

4. Alex works 4 hours on Tuesday, Thursday, and Friday. He earns $6.50 per hour. He is saving to buy a television that costs $525. How many weeks will Alex have to work to buy the television?

_____

_____

Choose a strategy to solve each problem.

5. You can buy a car for $3,500 in a state with no sales tax. The same car sells for 7% less in a state with a 7% sales tax. Which is the better buy?

_____

_____

6. A store is selling a sweater on sale for $17.90. The regular price is $22.95. What percent of the regular price is the sweater on sale for?

_____

_____

Reteaching 7-1

- The *mean* of a set of data is the sum of the values divided by the number of data items.

  $74 + 77 + 80 + 81 + 85 + 87 + 94 + 94 = 672$

  $672 \div 8 = 84$

  The mean math test grade is 84.

- The *median* of a data set is the middle value when the data are arranged in numerical order. When the grades are arranged in order from least to greatest, there are two middle numbers.

  74, 77, 80, 81, 85, 87, 94, 94

  To find the median, add the two middle numbers and divide the total by 2.

  $81 + 85 = 166$

  $166 \div 2 = 83$

  The median grade is 83.

Math Test Grades	
Sharon	81
Rashid	94
Durrin	77
Nicole	80
Terry	74
Mei-lin	94
Kevin	87
Carlos	85

- The *mode* of a data set is the item in the data set that appears most often. For this data, 94 is the mode.

Find the mean of each data set.

1. 8, 6, 5, 9, 7, 13

2. 12, 10, 16, 14, 8, 24

3. 9, 12, 14, 6, 8, 5

4. 104, 126, 128, 100, 97

5. 86, 68, 70, 48, 66, 76

6. 65, 50, 95, 35, 75, 100

Find the median of each data set.

7. 5, 4, 7, 9, 8

8. 12, 16, 19, 14, 14, 18

9. 9, 19, 21, 13

10. 46, 38, 22, 48, 61

11. 60, 57, 53, 78, 44, 51

12. 8, 6, 6, 5, 8, 9

Find the mode of each data set.

13. 3, 4, 5, 5, 3, 5, 4, 2

14. 1, 2, 1, 1, 2, 2, 3, 1

15. 6, 8, 3, 8, 3, 9, 3

16. 33, 35, 34, 33, 35, 33

17. 98, 97, 98, 98, 97

18. 110, 121, 121, 110, 115, 117, 119

Name _____ Class _____ Date _____

Practice 7-1

Mean, Median, and Mode

Find the mean, median, and mode of each data set.

1. 85, 91, 76, 85, 93 _____

2. 72, 76, 73, 74, 75 _____

3. $\frac{1}{2}, \frac{3}{8}, \frac{1}{16}, \frac{1}{2}, \frac{5}{8}, \frac{3}{8}, \frac{11}{16}, \frac{3}{8}$ _____

4. $\frac{2}{3}, \frac{8}{9}, \frac{1}{3}, \frac{5}{18}, \frac{2}{3}, \frac{7}{9}, \frac{1}{18}, \frac{1}{3}, \frac{1}{6}$ _____

5. 86.4, 87.2, 95.7, 96.4, 88.1, 94.9. 98.5, 94.8 _____

Use the tables for Exercises 6–11.

6. What is the mean height of the active volcanoes listed to the nearest foot?

   _____

7. What is the median height of the active volcanoes listed?

   _____

8. What is the mode of the heights of the active volcanoes listed?

   _____

9. What is the mean of the wages listed?

   _____

10. What is the median of the wages listed?

    _____

11. What is the mode of the wages listed?

    _____

Active Volcanoes	
Name	Height Above Sea Level (ft)
Cameroon Mt.	13,354
Mount Erebus	12,450
Asama	8,300
Gerde	9,705
Sarychev	5,115
Ometepe	5,106
Fogo	9,300
Mt. Hood	11,245
Lascar	19,652

Hourly Wages of Production Workers 1991 (includes benefits)	
Country	Wage
Austria	$17.47
Brazil	$2.55
Finland	$20.57
France	$15.26
Hong Kong	$3.58
Japan	$14.41
Mexico	$2.17
Spain	$12.65
United States	$15.45

Each student in a class has taken five tests. The teacher allows the students to pick the mean, median, or mode of each set of scores to be their average. Which average should each student pick in order to have the highest average?

12. 100, 87, 81, 23, 19 _____

13. 90, 80, 74, 74, 72 _____

14. 80, 80, 70, 67, 68 _____

15. 75, 78, 77, 70, 70 _____

16. 100, 47, 45, 32, 31 _____

17. 86, 86, 77, 14, 12 _____

18. 79, 78, 77, 76, 85 _____

19. 86, 80, 79, 70, 70 _____

108 Lesson 7-1 Practice

Course 1 Chapter 7

Reteaching 7-2

Organizing and Displaying Data

Sixteen students were asked to name their favorite school day. A *frequency table* can be used to organize their responses.

Favorite School Day	Tally	Frequency
Monday	III	3
Tuesday	II	2
Wednesday	III	3
Thursday	IIII	4
Friday	IIII	4

To make a frequency table:

① List all the choices.

② Mark a tally for each student's response.

③ Total the tallies for each choice.

Students compared the number of books they carry to school. A *line plot* can be used to show this data. Each ✗ represents one student.

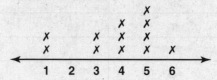

Number of Books Carried to School

To use a line plot to find the *range:*

① Subtract the least value from the greatest value along the horizontal line.

② The range is 6 − 1 or 5 books.

Organize each set of data by making a frequency table.

1. first letters of students' names:
   A, A, B, D, F, F, H, J, J, J, J

First Letter	Tally	Frequency
A		
B		
D		
F		
H		
J		

2. birthday months: March, May, April, June, July, June, May, May, May, July, March, May

Month	Tally	Frequency
March		
April		
May		
June		
July		

Make a line plot for each set of data. Find the range.

3. ages of middle school students:
   11, 12, 12, 12, 12, 12, 13, 13, 13, 13, 13, 13, 14, 14, 14

4. questions answered correctly on a quiz: 9, 9, 8, 7, 10, 9, 6, 7, 9, 9, 10, 8, 8, 8, 7, 6, 10, 10

The range is _____.

The range is _____.

Practice 7-2

1. **a.** Choose a page from a book you are reading. Choose 50 words on that page. Using these 50 words, complete the frequency table.

Letter	Tally	Frequency
t		
s		
r		
n		
d		

   b. Make a line plot for your frequency table.

   c. Which letter occurred most frequently in your sample? least frequently?

Use the line plot at the right for Exercises 2–5.

2. What information is displayed in the line plot?

   _____

3. How many students spent time doing homework last night?

   _____

4. How many students spent at least half an hour on homework?

   _____

5. What is the range of time spent on homework last night?

   _____

**Time Spent Doing
Homework Last Night
(min)**

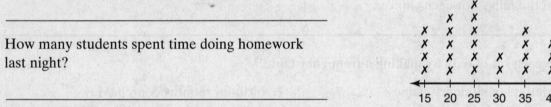

6. A kennel is boarding dogs that weigh the following amounts (in pounds).

5	62	43	48	12	17	29	74
8	15	4	11	15	26	63	

   a. What is the range of the dogs' weights?

   _____

   b. How many of the dogs weigh under 50 pounds?

   _____

Reteaching 7-3

Some problems contain many pieces of data.

Read and Understand	A stadium sells buttons, pins, and pennants. The prices are $1.25 for a button, $.54 for a pin, and $4.39 for a pennant. Audrey wants to buy an equal number of each. What is the greatest number she can buy without spending more than $20.00?
Plan and Solve	To solve the problem, it may help to make an organized list of prices. Stop when the total is close to but not more than $20.00.

	1	2	3	4
Buttons	$1.25	$2.50	$3.75	$5.00
Pins	$.54	$1.08	$1.62	$2.16
Pennants	$4.39	$8.78	$13.17	$17.56
Total	$6.18	$12.36	**$18.54**	$24.72

Audrey can buy 3 of each without spending more than $20.00.

Look Back and Check	You can estimate to check whether your answer is reasonable. *$4 + $2 + $13 is less than $20.*

Solve each problem by making an organized list.

1. On day one at your new babysitting job, you earn $2. On each day after that you will earn $.50 more than you did the day before. On what day will you earn $6.50?

   _____

2. How many ways can you make $.50 using nickels and dimes?

   _____

3. A bakery has four types of bread, A, B, C, and D and four types of meat, E, F, G, and H. How many bread-meat combinations can a customer choose from? Only one meat per bread type can be selected.

   _____

4. A library charges $.50 the first day and $.05 each additional day a book is overdue. Sonja paid an overdue fee of $2.15. How many days was the book overdue?

   _____

Practice 7-3

Solve each problem by making an organized list.

1. How many ways are possible to make change for 36¢?

    _____

2. Tom has a $20 bill, a $10 bill, a $5 bill, and a $1 bill. List the total
    costs possible for items he could buy if he receives no change.

    _____

3. A club began with 4 members. At each meeting every member
    must bring 2 new people. These new people become members.
    How many members will there be at the fourth meeting?

    _____

4. Colleen is making raffle tickets for the school's give-away
    drawing. She wants to use the digits 2, 5, and 7 to make three-
    digit numbers. How many different three-digit numbers can she
    make if she uses each digit once?

    _____

Choose a strategy to solve each problem.

5. Gavin sells popcorn at basketball games. A large box costs $.75,
    and a small box costs $.40. One night he sold 45 boxes and
    collected a total of $25. How many large and how many small
    boxes of popcorn did Gavin sell?

    _____

6. How many triangles are in the
    figure below.

    _____

    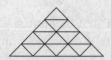

7. How many squares are in the floor
    tile below?

    _____

8. Find the smallest number that meets all of these conditions. _____

    *   when you divide the number by 5 there are 3 left over

    *   when you divide the number by 8 there are 2 left over

    *   when you divide the number by 9 there are 4 left over

Reteaching 7-4

Bar Graphs and Line Graphs

A *bar graph* uses vertical or horizontal bars to display numerical information. The length of the bars tell you the numbers they represent. To read the graph at the right, first read the horizontal axis. Then read from the top of a bar to the vertical axis. This graph shows that in September, an English class read 25 books. A *histogram* is a bar graph that shows the frequency of each data item.

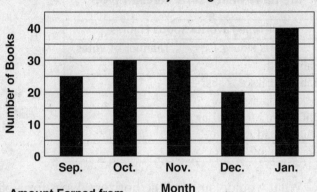

Books Read by an English Class

A *line graph* is a graph that uses a series of line segments to show changes in data. Usually, a line graph shows changes over time. For example, it may show a pattern of increase, decrease, or no change over time.

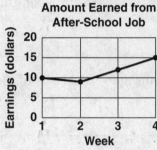

Amount Earned from After-School Job

Use the bar graph above for Exercises 1–4.

1. How many books were read in December?

   _____

2. In which month did students read the most books?

   _____

3. How many more books were read in January than in October?

   _____

4. In which two months did students read the same number of books?

   _____

Use the tables at the right for Exercises 5–6.

5. Would you use a bar graph, a histogram, or a line graph to display the data in the Sports table? Explain your choice.

   _____

   _____

Favorite Sports	
Sport	**Number Answering**
Wrestling	290
Football	50
Basketball	520
Baseball	130

6. Would you use a bar graph, a histogram, or a line graph for the Population data? Explain.

   _____

   _____

Population of Springdale	
Year	**Population**
1970	45,000
1980	62,000
1990	68,000

Practice 7-4

Use the table below for Exercises 1–3.

All-Time Favorite Sports Figures	
Sports Figure	**Number of Votes**
Babe Ruth	29
Babe Didrikson Zaharias	22
Jackie Robinson	18
Billie Jean Moffitt King	17
Muhammad Ali	14
Jim Thorpe	13

1. What would you label the horizontal axis for a bar graph of the data?

   _____

2. What interval would you use for the vertical axis of the bar graph?

   _____

3. Construct a bar graph displaying the number of votes for all-time favorite sports figures.

Use the table below for Exercises 4–5.

Daily Use of Petroleum in the U.S. (millions of barrels)									
Year	1950	1955	1960	1965	1970	1975	1980	1985	1990
Number	6.5	8.5	9.8	11.5	14.7	16.3	17.1	15.7	16.9

4. Make a line graph for the amount of petroleum used daily in the U.S.

5. What does the line graph show?

   _____

Use the table below for Exercises 6–7.

Time to Walk to School															
Time (min.)	1	2	3	4	5	6	7	8	9	10	11	12	13	14	15
Tally			II	IIII	III	IIII	I	II			I	I			I

6. Would the data be better displayed on a histogram with 3-minute intervals or 5-minute intervals? Explain.

   _____

7. Make a histogram for the time it takes a group of students to walk to school.

Reteaching 7-5

A *circle graph* is a graph of data where the entire circle represents the whole. Each wedge in the circle represents part of the whole. The graph at the right shows that 27 people in the survey speak English at home.

Languages Spoken at Home

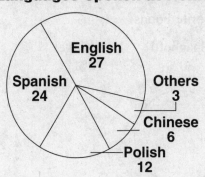

Use the circle graph above for Exercises 1–4.

1. Which 2 languages did most people surveyed speak?

_____

2. How many people spoke Polish?

_____

3. How many more people spoke Spanish than Polish?

_____

4. Did more people speak Polish or Chinese?

_____

Sketch a circle graph for the given percents.

5. 65%, 35%

6. 26%, 62%, 12%

7. 16%, 51%, 33%

8. 10%, 90%

9. 30%, 50%, 20%

10. 15%, 15%, 70%

Shade the circle graphs with a section equal to the given fraction.

11. $\frac{1}{4}$

12. $\frac{2}{3}$

13. $\frac{4}{5}$

Practice 7-5

Sketch a circle graph for the given percents.

1. Favorite Foods

Pizza	Spaghetti	Hamburger
60%	30%	10%

2. Favorite Type of Book

Animal	Sports	Adventure	Mystery
20%	25%	10%	45%

3. Favorite Color

Blue	Purple	Red
40%	35%	25%

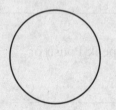

4. Favorite Sport

Swimming	Softball	Soccer	Hockey
20%	30%	5%	45%

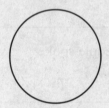

5. Number of TV Stations Received
by Homes

1–6	7–10	11–14	15–40	41–60
7%	34%	34%	19%	6%

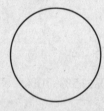

6. Bowling Record

Games Won	Games Lost	Games Tied	Forfeits
50%	35%	5%	10%

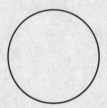

Use the circle graph for Exercises 7–9.

7. Which element is found in the greatest quantity in the body?

_____

8. List the three elements, from least to greatest quantity.

_____

9. Why might there be a portion labeled "other"?

_____

_____

**Major Elements Found
in the Body**

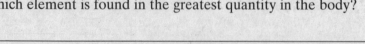

Reteaching 7-6

Party Pals has party equipment for rent. The company uses a *spreadsheet* to keep track of the number of hours its equipment is rented.

	A	B	C	D	E	F
1	Machine	Fri.	Sat.	Sun.	Total	Mean Rental Time
2	Party Popcorner	4	8	6		
3	Juice Fountain	0	3	3		
4	Soft Ice Cream Machine	8	9	4		
5	Pretzel Oven	1	6	5		

- A *cell* is a box in a spreadsheet where a particular row and column meet. In column C, you find the cells C1, C2, C3, and so on. C2 shows 8. Its value is 8 hours.

- Missing values can be found by telling the spreadsheet what calculation to do. The value for cell E3 can be found by using the formula = B3 + C3 + D3.

Use the spreadsheet above for Exercises 1–13. Identify the cell(s) that indicate each category.

1. machines rented

_____

2. rental times for Saturday

_____

3. total rental hours for the Popcorner

_____

4. mean rental time for the pretzel oven

_____

Write the value for the given cell.

5. B5

_____

6. C4

_____

7. D3

_____

8. B3

_____

9. D5

_____

Write a formula to find each quantity.

10. the total in cell E4

_____

11. the total in cell E5

_____

12. the total in cell E2

_____

13. the mean score in cell F5

_____

Practice 7-6

Gervase works after school and on weekends at a pet store, where he is paid $5 per hour. He uses the following spreadsheet to keep track of the time he works and the money he earns.

	A	B	C	D	E
1	Day	Time In (P.M.)	Time Out (P.M.)	Hours Worked	Amount Earned
2	Monday	4	7		
3	Tuesday	4	7		
4	Thursday	4	8		
5	Saturday	1	9		
6			Total		

Write the value for the given cell. What does the number represent?

1. D2

   _____

2. E2

   _____

3. D3

   _____

4. E3

   _____

5. D4

   _____

6. E4

   _____

Write a formula to find the value of each cell.

7. D5

   _____

8. E5

   _____

9. D6

   _____

10. E6

    _____

11. How many hours does Gervase work in a week?

    _____

12. How much does Gervase earn in a week?

    _____

13. Rosario worked for $14.50 an hour on the weekdays and $15.25 an hour on the weekends. On Monday she worked 3 hours, on Tuesday she worked 5 hours, and on Saturday and Sunday she worked 8 hours each day.

    a. Make a spreadsheet similar to the one above. Use column B for hourly wage, column C for hours worked, and column D for amount earned.

    b. How much money did Rosario make each day and at the end of one week?

    _____

    _____

Reteaching 7-7

Stem-and-Leaf Plots

A *stem-and-leaf plot* is a graph that uses the digits of each number to show the shape of the data. Each data value is broken into a "stem" on the left and a "leaf" on the right. A vertical segment separates the stems from the leaves. To read the data, combine the stem with each leaf in the same row.

Example: Make a stem-and-leaf diagram of the data showing minutes spent eating lunch.

Minutes Spent Eating Lunch
46, 35, 12, 37, 28, 10, 22, 54, 19, 13, 46, 51

① Decide what the stem of the diagram will represent. Since these data are two-digit numbers, the stem will be the tens digits and the leaves will be the ones digits.

② Write the tens digits in order in the lefthand column of the diagram. Then write each leaf at the right of its stem as they occur in the problem.

③ Complete the second stem-and-leaf diagram, with the leaves in order from least to greatest.

②

Stem	Leaf
1	2 0 9 3
2	8 2
3	5 7
4	6 6
5	4 1

③

Stem	Leaf
1	0 2 3 9
2	2 8
3	5 7
4	6 6
5	1 4

For Exercises 1–4, use the stem-and-leaf plot at the right.

1. What does 1 | 8 represent?

   _____

2. How many entries have a value of 25?

   _____

3. How many people were older than 40?

   _____

4. How many people were at the poetry reading?

   _____

5. Make a stem-and-leaf plot for the data showing the monthly attendance at the teen club.

Ages of People Attending a Poetry Reading

Stem	Leaf
0	5 8 8 9
1	8 8 9 9
2	3 5 5 6 8 8 9
3	2 2 7
4	0 1 3
5	2 8
6	4 4 6 7 8

Key 0 | 8 means 8 years old

Attendance at Teen Club
489, 527, 479, 519, 514, 480, 493, 523, 508, 504

Stem	Leaf

Practice 7-7

Use the stem-and-leaf plot for Exercises 1–7.

Ages of Grandparents	
stem	leaf
6	7 8 8
7	0 1 2 3 4 9 9
8	1 3 3 3 4 7
9	0 2 5

1. What is the age of the youngest grandparent? _____

2. What is the age of the oldest grandparent? _____

3. How many grandparents are 79 years old? _____

4. How many grandparents are older than 74? _____

5. What is the range of the data? _____

6. What is the median? _____

7. What is the mode? _____

Make a stem-and-leaf plot for each set of data.

8. scores on a history test

84, 93, 72, 87, 86, 97, 68, 74, 86, 91, 64, 83, 79, 80, 72, 83, 76, 90, 77

stem	leaf

9. number of badges earned by local scouts

7, 12, 9, 2, 17, 24, 0, 3, 10, 20, 12, 3, 6, 4, 9, 15

stem	leaf

10. minutes to travel to a friend's house

12, 31, 5, 10, 23, 17, 21, 12, 8, 33, 3, 11, 10, 25, 9, 16

stem	leaf

Reteaching 7-8

Data can be displayed on graphs in ways that are misleading.

The horizontal scales make these line graphs seem different.

As the numbers are moved farther apart, it appears that the change over time is less.

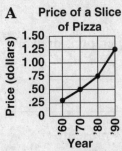

A   Price of a Slice of Pizza

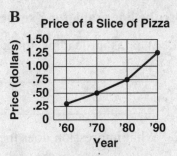

B   Price of a Slice of Pizza

These bar graphs may seem different because of how the vertical scales are drawn.

The break in the vertical scale makes the differences seem greater than they really are.

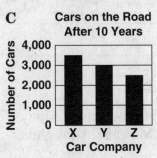

C   Cars on the Road After 10 Years

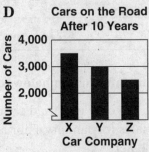

D   Cars on the Road After 10 Years

Use the graphs above for Exercises 1–4.

1. Which graph might be used to convince someone that the price of pizza has risen too quickly over the years?

   _____

2. Which graph might be used to convince someone that pizza makers should raise their prices?

   _____

3. Which graph would Car Company X use to show that its cars last longer than the competition?

   _____

4. Which graph of cars still on the road after 10 years would Car Company Z prefer?

   _____

5. On a science exam, six students scored a mean of 75. Their scores were 88, 90, 12, 85, 87, and 88. Why might the mean be misleading?

   _____

   _____

   _____

Practice 7-8

Use the line graph for Exercises 1–2.

1. What is misleading about the way the graph is drawn?

   _____

   _____

2. What impression does the graph try to present?

   _____

   _____

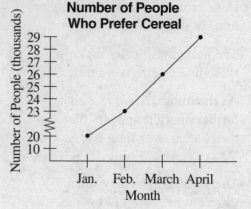

Number of People Who Prefer Cereal

Use the information below for Exercises 3–4.

There are only two used car dealers in Auto City. Monthly auto sales for January, February, and March are shown for one dealer.

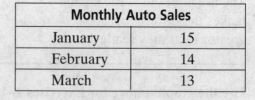

Monthly Auto Sales	
January	15
February	14
March	13

3. A competitor created the graph below.

   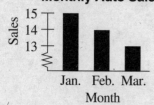

   Monthly Auto Sales

   a. What impression is given by the graph?

      _____

   b. Why is the graph misleading?

      _____

      _____

      _____

   c. Draw a line graph to accurately reflect the sales.

4. Suppose 15 cars sell in April and 10 cars in May.

   a. Would a salesman use the mean, median, or mode to make sales look greatest?

      _____

   b. Would the mean, median, or mode be used in an advertisement stating that sales are declining?

      _____

Reteaching 8-1

Points, Lines, Segments, and Rays

Each *point F, G*, and *H*, indicates an exact location in space.

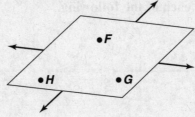

Plane FGH is flat and extends indefinitely as suggested by the arrows.

Line KM ($\overleftrightarrow{KM}$) is a series of points that extends in two opposite directions without end.

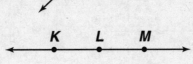

Segment LM ($\overline{LM}$) is part of $\overleftrightarrow{KM}$. The points *L* and *M* are endpoints of $\overline{LM}$.

Ray LM ($\overrightarrow{LM}$) is part of a line. Point *L* is its only endpoint.

$\overleftrightarrow{ST}$ and $\overleftrightarrow{UV}$ are *parallel lines*. They are in the same plane but do not intersect. They have no points in common.

Points on the same line are *collinear*. Points *S* and *T* are collinear.

Skew lines are neither parallel nor intersecting.

Read each statement. Write *true* or *false*.

1. A line has two endpoints.

    _____

2. A plane has only two points.

    _____

3. A segment is part of a line.

    _____

4. A plane is flat.

    _____

5. Collinear points lie on different lines.

    _____

6. A ray has two endpoints.

    _____

7. A ray has no beginning or end.

    _____

8. A plane contains only one line.

    _____

9. Parallel segments do not intersect.

    _____

10. Skew lines intersect.

    _____

Match each figure with its name.

11.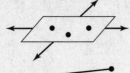

12.    _____

13. _____   14. _____

a. ray

b. plane

c. line

d. segment

Practice 8-1

Points, Lines, Segments, and Rays

Use the diagram at the right. Name each of the following.

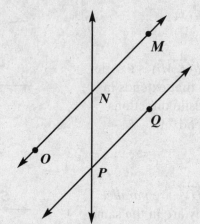

1. three collinear points

_____

2. three noncollinear points

_____

3. three segments

_____

4. three rays

_____

5. two lines that appear to be parallel

_____

6. two pairs of intersecting lines

_____

7. Draw four collinear points.

8. Draw five noncollinear points.

Use *sometimes*, *always*, or *never* to complete each sentence.

9. Three points are _____
collinear.

10. Four points are _____
noncollinear.

11. A ray _____ has one
endpoint.

12. A line _____ has an
endpoint.

Name the segments that appear to be parallel.

13.

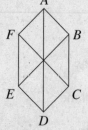

14.

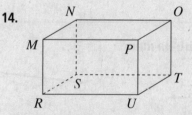

_____

_____

Reteaching 8-2

You can classify an *angle* according to its measure in degrees.

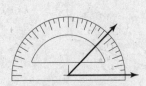

between 0° and 90°
acute angle

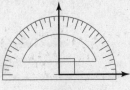

90°
right angle

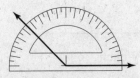

between 90° and 180°
obtuse angle

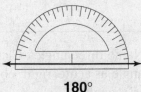

180°
straight angle

Classifying can help you estimate and measure the size of ∠*RST*.

∠*RST* is an obtuse angle.
It is greater than 90° but less than 180°.
A good estimate is 135°.

To find the measure of ∠*RST*:

① Extend the sides so they reach the scales on the *protractor*.

② Place the protractor over the angle as shown. $\overrightarrow{ST}$ is on zero.

③ Read the inner scale.

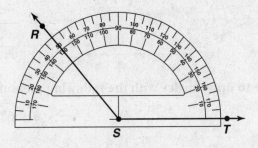

The measure of ∠*RST* is 130°. Since ∠*RST* is obtuse, it cannot be 50°.

Classify each angle as *acute*, *right*, *obtuse*, or *straight*.

1.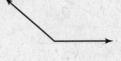

2.

3.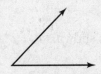

4.

_____   _____   _____   _____

Use a protractor to measure each angle.

5.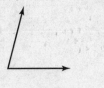

6.

7.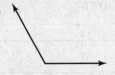

8.

_____   _____   _____   _____

Practice 8-2

Use the diagram at the right.

1. Name three rays.

   _____

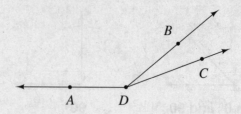

2. Name three angles. Classify each angle as acute, right, obtuse, or straight.

   _____

Measure each angle with a protractor.

3. _____

4. _____

5. _____

6. _____

Use a protractor to draw angles with the following measures.

7. 88°

8. 66°

Use the diagram at the right.

9. Use a protractor to measure ∠MSN, ∠NSO, ∠OSP, ∠PSQ, and ∠QSR.

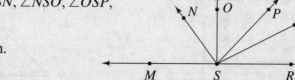

10. List all of the obtuse angles shown.

    _____

11. List all of the right angles shown.

    _____

12. List all the straight angles shown.

    _____

13. List all the acute angles shown.

    _____

    _____

14. What are the angle measures in the figure shown at the right?

    _____

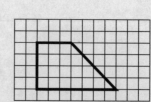

Reteaching 8-3

Complementary angles:
sum of measures = 90°.

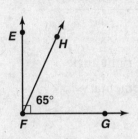

Example 1: Find the
complement of ∠HFG.

$x + 65° = 90°$

$x = 25°$

∠EFH has a measure of 25°.

Supplementary angles:
sum of measures = 180°.

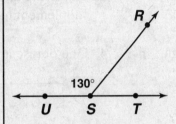

Example 2: Find the
supplement of ∠USR.

$x + 130° = 180°$

$x = 50°$

∠RST has a measure of 50°.

Congruent angles
have the same measure.

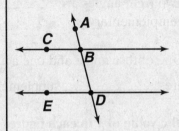

Example 3: ∠ABC and ∠BDE
have the same measure; they
are congruent.

Find the value of x in each figure.

1.

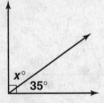

_____

2.

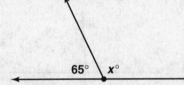

_____

3.

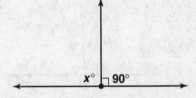

_____

**Use the diagram at the right. Complete each sentence with *complementary*,
supplementary, or *congruent*. Some exercises use more than one word.**

4. Angles 1 and 2 are

   _____.

5. Angles 9 and 10 are

   _____.

6. Angles 3 and 7 are

   _____.

7. Angles 4 and 5 are

   _____.

8. Angles 10 and 11 are

   _____.

9. Angles 7 and 14 are

   _____.

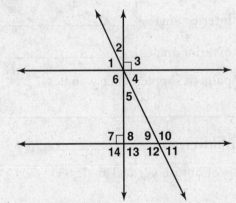

Practice 8-3

Special Pairs of Angles

Complete each sentence with *sometimes*, *always*, or *never*.

1. Two right angles are _____ complementary.

2. Two acute angles are _____ supplementary.

3. One obtuse angle and one acute angle are _____ supplementary.

4. One obtuse angle and one right angle are _____ supplementary.

Find the value of *x* in each figure.

5.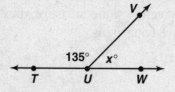

6.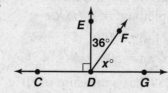

7.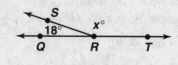

_____ _____ _____

8.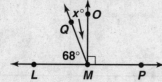

9.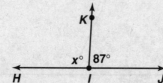

10.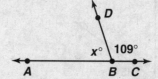

_____ _____ _____

Use the diagram at the right to identify each of the following.

11. two interior angles _____

12. two exterior angles _____

13. two pairs of supplementary angles

_____

14. the transversal _____

15. a pair of obtuse vertical angles

_____

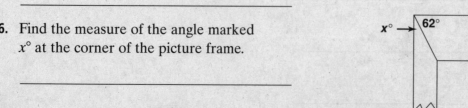

16. Find the measure of the angle marked
    x° at the corner of the picture frame.

_____

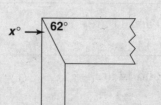

Reteaching 8-4

Classifying Triangles

Triangles can be classified by the measures of their angles.

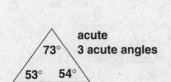

acute
3 acute angles

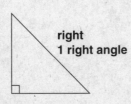

right
1 right angle

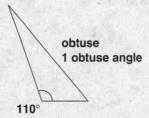

obtuse
1 obtuse angle

Triangles can be classified by the number of congruent sides.

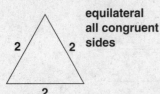

equilateral
all congruent
sides

isosceles
2 congruent
sides

scalene
no congruent
sides

Classify each triangle as *acute, right,* or *obtuse.*

1.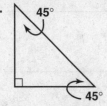

2.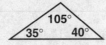

3.

4.

_____   _____   _____   _____

Classify each triangle by its angles.

5. 90°, 40°, 50°   **6.** 38°, 72°, 70°   **7.** 115°, 30°, 35°   **8.** 70°, 60°, 50°

_____   _____   _____   _____

Classify each triangle by its sides.

9.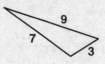

10.

11.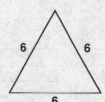

12.

_____   _____   _____   _____

Practice 8-4

Measure the sides and angles of each triangle. Then name each triangle by its angles and its sides.

1.

2.

3.

_____   _____   _____

Choose the best description for each triangle with the following side lengths.

4. 8, 9, 8 _____

5. 3, 4, 5 _____

6. 15, 15, 15 _____

7. 4, 7, 9 _____

Choose the best description for each triangle with the following angles.

8. 60°, 60°, 60°

_____

9. 25°, 14°, 141°

_____

10. 90°, 63°, 27°

_____

11. 90°, 89°, 1°

_____

Sketch each triangle. If you cannot sketch a triangle, explain why.

12. a right obtuse triangle

13. an acute equilateral triangle

14. an isosceles scalene triangle

_____   _____   _____

_____   _____   _____

_____   _____   _____

_____   _____   _____

Name _____ Class _____ Date _____

Reteaching 8-5

Exploring and Classifying Polygons

A *polygon* is a closed figure formed by three or more line segments that do not cross.

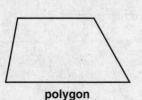

polygon

not
closed

not a
line
segment

not polygons

segments

cross

Polygons can be named according to the number of sides.

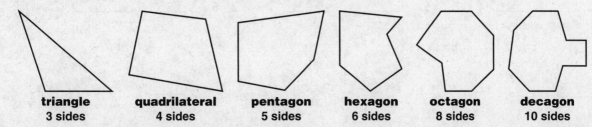

| triangle | quadrilateral | pentagon | hexagon | octagon | decagon |
| 3 sides | 4 sides | 5 sides | 6 sides | 8 sides | 10 sides |

Write all the possible names for each quadrilateral. Choose from
parallelogram, rhombus, square,* and *trapezoid.

1.

2.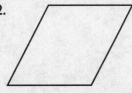

3.

4.

_____   _____   _____   _____

_____   _____   _____   _____

_____   _____   _____   _____

Identify each polygon according to the number of sides.

5.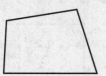

6.

7.

8.

_____   _____   _____   _____

9.

10.

11.

12.

_____   _____   _____   _____

Practice 8-5

Exploring and Classifying Polygons

Identify each polygon according to the number of sides.

1. _____

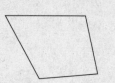

2. _____

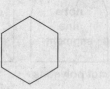

3. _____

4. _____

5. _____

6. _____

Use the dot paper below to draw an example of each polygon.

7. a quadrilateral with one right angle

8. a pentagon with no right angle

9. a hexagon with two right angles

Use the diagram to identify all the polygons for each name.

10. quadrilateral

_____

11. parallelogram

_____

12. rhombus

_____

13. rectangle

_____

14. square

_____

15. trapezoid

_____

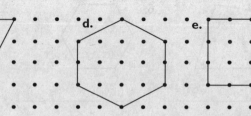

Reteaching 8-6

Daniel, Sandy, Rita, and Joseph mixed up their class schedules. Each student has math class during a different period, and the schedules show math in period A, B, C, or D. Daniel knows he eats lunch during period C. Sandy sees Daniel arrive for math class just as she is leaving. Rita goes to math after eating lunch with Daniel. Which schedule belongs to each student?

Read and Understand

There are four different schedules for four students. Clues are given about which schedule belongs to each student. The goal is to match each student with a schedule.

Plan and Solve

Make a table. Label the schedules A, B, C, and D for the periods in which math appears. Use the clues to determine whether or not a student has a given schedule.

	A	B	C	D
Daniel	No	Yes	No	No
Sandy	Yes	No	No	No
Rita	No	No	No	Yes
Joseph	No	No	Yes	No

- Daniel eats lunch during period C. Write "No" in the box for Daniel and schedule C.

- Rita goes to math after eating lunch with Daniel. Rita must have math during period D.

- Sandy sees Daniel arrive for math just as she is leaving. To have math before Daniel, Sandy must go to math in period A. Daniel has math in period B.

- Complete the table. Joseph must have math in period C.

Look Back and Check

Reread the problem. Make sure your solution matches all the facts given.

Solve each problem using logical reasoning.

1. Patrick, Tony, and Neil live in a row of three houses on the same street. Walking past their houses, they pass a white house first, then a green house, then a blue house. Patrick lives next door to the green house. Tony does not live next door to his friend who lives in the blue house. Who lives in each house?

   _____

   _____

2. A landscaper is planting five types of flowers in a row. The daisies are not planted at either end of the row. The snapdragons are planted at one of the ends and are next to the daffodils. The tulips are only next to the hyacinths. The hyacinths are second in the row. In what order did the landscaper plant the flowers?

   _____

   _____

Practice 8-6

Problem Solving: Use Logical Reasoning

Solve each problem using logical reasoning. Show your work.

1. A local restaurant features a three-course meal. For the first
course, you can choose from soup, salad, cottage cheese, or
coleslaw. For the second course, you can choose from beef, pork,
chicken, or a vegetarian pasta dish. For the third course, you can
choose from sherbet, rice pudding, or ice cream. How many
different meals could you choose if you choose one item from
each course?

_____

2. In a sixth-grade class of 28 students, 23 like to watch basketball.
Also, 15 like to watch baseball. Twelve in the class said they like
to watch both sports. How many students in the class do not like
to watch either sport?

_____

Use any strategy to solve each problem. Show your work.

3. Don has a pile of pennies. When he separates the pennies into
stacks of two, he has one left over. When he separates the
pennies into stacks of five, he has four left over. When he
separates the pennies into stacks of seven, he has none left over.
What is the least number of pennies that Don could have?

_____

4. Mara bought some flowers to plant in her garden. When she
separated the plants into groups of three or five, she had one
plant left over. When she separated the plants into groups of
eight, she had none left over. What is the smallest number of
plants that Mara could have bought?

_____

5. Use the clues to make a 4-by-4 word square.

   a. a triangle has three

   b. a thought or opinion

   c. where lions sleep

   d. opposite of west

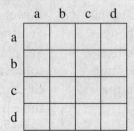

Name _____ Class _____ Date _____

Reteaching 8-7

Congruent figures have the same size and shape. Matching sides and matching angles are congruent. These are corresponding parts. Here, quadrilaterals *ABCD* and *EFGH* are congruent.

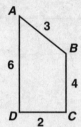 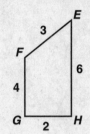

Similar figures have the same shape, but may not be the same size. They have congruent corresponding angles and proportional corresponding sides. Here, triangles *RST* and *UVW* are similar.

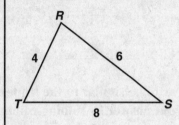 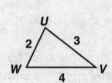

For each triangle, tell whether it is congruent to triangle *RST*.

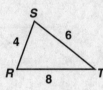

1.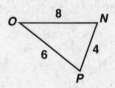

_____

2.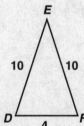

_____

3.

_____

4. List the figures that are similar to the figure shown.

a.

b.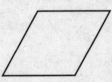

c.

Tell whether the figures are *congruent* or *similar*.

5.

_____

6.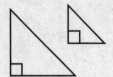

_____

7.

_____

Practice 8-7

Congruent and Similar Figures

• •

For each figure tell whether it is congruent to the parallelogram at the right.

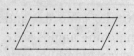

1. 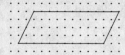 **2.**  **3.** 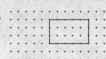 **4.**

_____ _____ _____ _____

Which trapezoids appear to be similar to the trapezoid at the right? Confirm your answer by finding whether corresponding sides are proportional.

5. 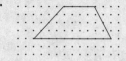 **6.**  **7.**  **8.**

_____ _____ _____ _____

Tell whether the triangles are *congruent*, *similar*, or *neither*.

9.   **10.**  **11.**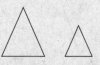

_____ _____ _____

12. List the pairs of figures that appear to be similar.

_____

a.   **b.**   **c.**   **d.**

e.   **f.**   **g.**   **h.**

13. The figure below contains eight congruent triangles. Redraw the figure with four fewer segments, so that only four congruent triangles remain.

Name _____ Class _____ Date _____

Reteaching 8-8

A figure has *line symmetry* if you can fold it in half so that the two halves match exactly. The line is called a *line of symmetry.*

This figure has line symmetry.
Trace the figure and the line through it.
Cut out the figure and fold it on the line.
The two halves match exactly.

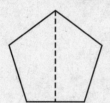

This figure *does not have* line symmetry.
Trace the figure and the line through it.
Cut out the figure and fold it on the line
(or on any other line). The two halves do
not match exactly.

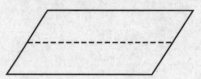

Some figures have many lines of symmetry. Draw a circle and try to
find all the lines of symmetry.

**Does the figure have line symmetry? Write *yes* or *no*. If yes, trace the
figure and draw all the lines of symmetry.**

1.

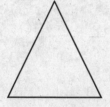

_____

2.

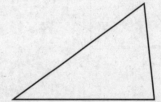

_____

3.

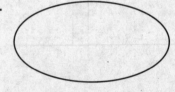

_____

4.

_____

5.

_____

6.

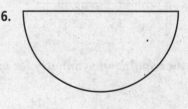

_____

**Can you find a line of symmetry for each word? Write *yes* or *no*. If
yes, copy the word and draw the line of symmetry.**

7. DAD   8. HAH   9. DAY   10. COB

_____   _____   _____   _____

Practice 8-8

Tell whether each figure has line symmetry. If it does, draw the line(s) of symmetry. If not, write *none*.

1.

2.

3.

4.

5.

6.

Complete each figure so that the line is a line of symmetry.

7.
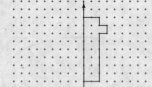

8.
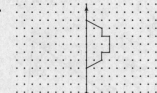

9.
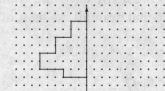

10.
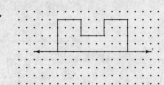

11.
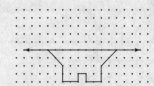

12.

Is there a line of symmetry for each word? If so, draw it.

13.
BOX

14.
TOOT

15.
CHICO

16.
MOM

17. Many logos such as the one at the right have both horizontal line symmetry and vertical line symmetry. Design three other logos, one with horizontal line symmetry only, one with vertical line symmetry only, and one with both horizontal and vertical line symmetry.

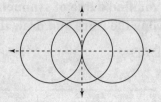

Name _____ Class _____ Date _____

Reteaching 8-9

In a *translation,* or slide, every point of a figure moves the same distance and in the same direction.

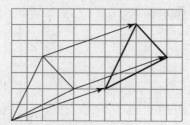

In a *reflection,* or flip, a figure is flipped across a line. The new figure is a mirror image of the original figure.

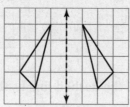

In a *rotation,* a figure is turned, or rotated about a point. You can describe a rotation in terms of degrees. The triangle has been rotated 90° clockwise.

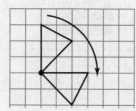

Draw a translation of each triangle.

1.
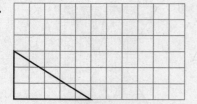

2.
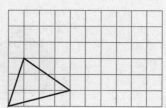

Copy each triangle. Draw its reflection over the given line.

3.
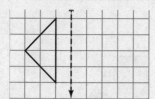

4.
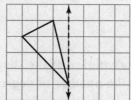

Circle all rotations of the first shape. State the number of degrees you must rotate the shape.

5.   a.   b.   c.

Practice 8-9

Draw two translations of each figure.

1.

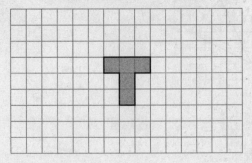

2.

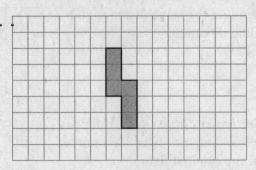

Draw the reflection of each figure. Use the dashed line as the line of reflection.

3.

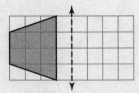

4.

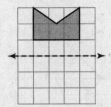

5.

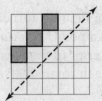

Tell whether each pair of figures shows a translation or a reflection.

6.

7.

8.

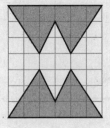

_____   _____   _____

Tell whether each figure is a rotation of the shape at the right.
Write *yes* or *no*. If so, state the number of degrees.

9.

10.

11.

12.

_____   _____   _____   _____

Reteaching 9-1

Metric Units of Length, Mass, and Capacity

The standard unit of length in the metric system is the *meter*.

millimeter (mm)	= 0.001 meter
centimeter (cm)	= 0.01 meter
meter (m)	= 1 meter
kilometer (km)	= 1,000 meters

A length can be named using different metric units. The point marked on the ruler is 2.7 centimeters.

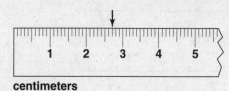

centimeters

Since each centimeter is 10 millimeters, the point is also 27 millimeters.

In the metric system, solids can be measured in units of *mass*.

milligram (mg)	= 0.001 gram
gram (g)	= 1 gram
kilogram (kg)	= 1,000 grams

The standard unit of mass is the *gram*.
- The mass of a vitamin pill may be measured in milligrams.
- A thumbtack has a mass of about 1 gram.
- A full liter bottle of soda has a mass of about 1 kilogram.

Liquids are measured in units of *capacity*.

milliliter (mL)	= 0.001 liter
liter (L)	= 1 liter
kiloliter (kL)	= 1,000 liters

The standard unit of capacity is the *liter*.
- The capacity of a soup spoon is measured in milliliters.
- A 1-liter soda bottle can fill about four average-sized glasses.
- Water in a river is measured in kiloliters.

Choose an appropriate metric unit of length.

1. distance across the end of a pencil _____

2. length of a thumb _____

3. distance from your home to Australia _____

4. width of a swimming pool _____

Choose an appropriate metric unit of mass.

5. the mass of a tooth _____

6. the mass of a puppy _____

Choose an appropriate metric unit of capacity.

7. the capacity of a bucket of water _____

8. the amount of water in a pond _____

Practice 9-1

Choose an appropriate metric unit of length.

1. the height of an office building

_____

2. the width of a page of a text

_____

3. the length of an ant

_____

4. the depth of a lake

_____

Use a metric ruler to find each length in millimeters and in centimeters.

5. ◄————————►

_____

6. ◄—————►

_____

7. ◄————————————►

_____

Choose an appropriate metric unit of mass.

8. a grain of rice

_____

9. a bag of groceries

_____

10. a feather

_____

11. a cat

_____

12. a leaf

_____

13. an eraser

_____

Choose an appropriate metric unit of capacity.

14. a gasoline tank

_____

15. a coffee mug

_____

16. 6 raindrops

_____

17. a pitcher of juice

_____

18. a swimming pool

_____

19. a can of paint

_____

Is each measurement reasonable? Write *True* or *False*.

20. The mass of the horse is about 500 kg.

_____

21. Jean drank 5.8 L of juice at breakfast.

_____

22. A mug holds 250 mL of hot chocolate.

_____

23. A penny is about 3 kg.

_____

24. A teaspoon holds about 5 L.

_____

25. A textbook is about 1 kg.

_____

26. The mass of a nail is about 500 g.

_____

27. A soccer field is about 5 m long.

_____

Reteaching 9-2

The most common metric units use the prefixes *kilo-*, *centi-*, and *milli-*.

Prefix	Meaning	Examples
kilo-	1,000	kilometer (1,000 m), kilogram (1,000 g), kiloliter (1,000 L)
centi-	$\frac{1}{100}$ or 0.01	centimeter (or 0.01 m), centigram (or 0.01 g), centiliter (or 0.01 L)
milli-	$\frac{1}{1,000}$ or 0.001	millimeter (or 0.001 m), milligram (or 0.001 g), milliliter (or 0.001 L)

Multiply to convert from larger units to smaller units.

Convert 4.7 kilometers to meters.

- A kilometer is larger than a meter. Multiply.

- Since 1 km = 1,000 m, multiply by 1,000.

$$4.7 \times 1,000 = 4,700$$
$$4.7 \text{ km} = 4,700 \text{ m}$$

- Or use mental math. Multiply by 1,000 by moving the decimal point three places to the *right*.

$$4.7 \rightarrow 4,700$$

Divide to convert from smaller units to larger units.

Convert 347 milliliters to liters.

- A milliliter is smaller than a liter. Divide.

- Since 1,000 mL = 1 L, divide by 1,000.

$$347 \div 1,000 = 0.347$$
$$347 \text{ mL} = 0.347 \text{ L}$$

- Or use mental math. Divide by 1,000 by moving the decimal point three places to the *left*.

$$347 \rightarrow 0.347$$

Convert each measurement to meters.

1. 2.5 km _____

2. 371 cm _____

3. 490 mm _____

4. 48 cm _____

5. 4 km _____

6. 1,500 mm _____

Convert each measurement to liters.

7. 0.6 kL _____

8. 799 cL _____

9. 0.9 mL _____

10. 35.6 mL _____

11. 0.006 kL _____

12. 1.8 cL _____

Convert each measurement to grams.

13. 4 kg _____

14. 661 cg _____

15. 1,500 mg _____

16. 2 cg _____

17. 1.95 kg _____

18. 2.3 mg _____

Convert each measurement.

19. 19 mL = _____ L

20. 5.5 kg = _____ g

21. 4.9 cL = _____ L

22. 730 mg = _____ g

23. 0.06 kL = _____ L

24. 2,540 mm = _____ cm

Practice 9-2

Converting Units in the Metric System

Convert each measurement to meters.

1. 800 mm
2. 50 cm
3. 2.6 km
4. 7 km
5. 250 mm

6. 35 km
7. 40 mm
8. 300 cm
9. 1.8 km
10. 450 cm

Convert each measurement to liters.

11. 160 mL
12. 0.36 kL
13. 0.002 kL
14. 240.9 mL
15. 368.5 mL

16. 8 kL
17. 80 mL
18. 17.3 mL
19. 0.09 kL
20. 330 mL

Convert each measurement to grams.

21. 4,000 mg
22. 7 kg
23. 56,000 mg
24. 0.19 kg
25. 754.8 mg

26. 600 mg
27. 90 kg
28. 2,800 mg
29. 0.4 kg
30. 58.1 mg

Convert each measurement.

31. _?_ km = 3,400 m
32. 420 mL = _?_ cL
33. 37 cm = _?_ m

34. 5,100 mg = _?_ cg
35. 77.8 mm = _?_ cm
36. 9.5 kL = _?_ L

37. 2.564 kg = _?_ g
38. _?_ m = 400,000 cm
39. 948 mm = _?_ cm

40. _?_ mL = 0.648 cL
41. _?_ kg = 6,000 g
42. _?_ L = 0.1678 kL

Reteaching 9-3

Perimeter

The *perimeter* of a figure is the sum of the lengths of its sides. Opposite sides of a rectangle are equal. To find the perimeter, add the 2 lengths (ℓ) and the 2 widths (w).

$$P = \ell + \ell + w + w \text{ or } P = 2\ell + 2w$$

Find the perimeter.

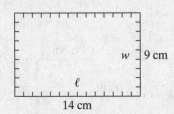

$$
\begin{aligned}
P &= 2\ell + 2w \\
&= 2(14) + 2(9) \\
&= 28 + 18 = 46
\end{aligned}
$$

The perimeter is 46 centimeters.

Area

The *area* of a figure is the number of square units needed to cover the figure. To find the area of a rectangle, multiply the length (ℓ) and the width (w).

$$A = \ell \times w$$

Find the area.

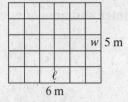

$$
\begin{aligned}
A &= \ell \times w \\
&= 6 \times 5 \\
&= 30
\end{aligned}
$$

The area is 30 square meters.

Estimate the area of each figure. Each square represents 1 square inch.

1.

_____

2.

_____

3.

_____

Find the perimeter and area of each rectangle or square.

4. $\ell = 12$ cm, $w = 2$ cm

5. $\ell = 9$ ft, $w = 7.5$ ft

6. $\ell = 2.5$ m, $w = 2.5$ m

_____   _____   _____

7. $\ell = 5.5$ in., $w = 5.5$ in.

8. $\ell = 6.2$ in., $w = 3.4$ in.

9. $\ell = 4.5$ ft, $w = 0.75$ ft

_____   _____   _____

10. $\ell = 8$ cm, $w = 8$ cm

11. $\ell = 10.5$ m, $w = 5.2$ m

12. $\ell = 22$ in., $w = 9$ in.

_____   _____   _____

13. What is the area of a square with a perimeter of 60 meters?

_____

Practice 9-3

Perimeters and Areas of Rectangles

Estimate the area of each figure. Each square represents 2 square inches.

1.
   _____

2.
   _____

3.
   _____

Find the perimeter and area of each rectangle.

4.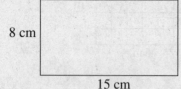
   8 cm, 15 cm
   _____

5.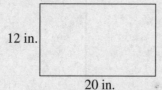
   12 in., 20 in.
   _____

6.
   6 cm, 6 cm
   _____

7. $\ell = 5$ in., $w = 13$ in.
   _____

8. $\ell = 18$ m, $w = 12$ m
   _____

9. $\ell = 3$ ft, $w = 8$ ft
   _____

Find the area of each square given the side s or the perimeter P.

10. $s = 3.5$ yd
    _____

11. $s = 9$ cm
    _____

12. $P = 24$ m
    _____

13. $P = 38$ in.
    _____

Choose a calculator, paper and pencil, or mental math to solve.

14. The length of a rectangle is 8 centimeters. The width is 6 centimeters.

    a. What is the area? _____ b. What is the perimeter? _____

15. The area of a rectangle is 45 square inches.
    One dimension is 5 inches. What is the perimeter? _____

16. The perimeter of a square is 36 centimeters.
    What is the area of the square? _____

17. The perimeter of a rectangle is 38 centimeters.
    The length is 7.5 centimeters. What is the width? _____

18. The figure at the right contains only squares.
    Each side of the shaded square is 1 unit.
    What is the length, width, and area of the figure?

    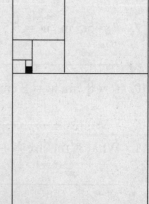

    _____

Reteaching 9-4

Parallelogram

To find the area of a parallelogram, multiply base times height.

$$A = b \times h$$

Find the area of the parallelogram.

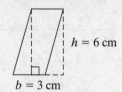

$h = 6$ cm

$b = 3$ cm

$$A = b \times h$$
$$= 3 \times 6$$
$$= 18$$

The area is 18 square centimeters.

Triangle

The area of a triangle is $\frac{1}{2}$ times the base times the height.

$$A = \frac{1}{2}b \times h$$

Find the area of the triangle.

$h = 6$ cm

$b = 3$ cm

$$A = \frac{1}{2} \times b \times h$$
$$= \frac{1}{2} \times 3 \times 6$$
$$= 9$$

The area is 9 square centimeters.

Find the area of each parallelogram.

1. $b = 6$ ft, $h = 8$ ft

2. $b = 12$ in, $h = 9$ in.

3. $b = 6$ yd, $h = 12$ yd

_____

4. $b = 2.8$ in., $h = 3.4$ in.

5. $b = 31$ yd, $h = 19$ yd

6. $b = 4.5$ m, $h = 4.5$ m

_____

7. $b = 15$ cm, $h = 7$ cm

8. $b = 8.3$ ft, $h = 11.7$ ft

9. $b = 14.4$ m, $h = 6.5$ m

_____

Find the area of each triangle.

10. $b = 8$ cm, $h = 14$ cm

11. $b = 7$ in., $h = 18$ in.

12. $b = 11$ m, $h = 4.6$ m

_____

13. $b = 6.4$ ft, $h = 3.5$ ft

14. $b = 104$ in., $h = 55$ in.

15. $b = 5.9$ cm, $h = 4.2$ cm

_____

16. $b = 1.7$ m, $h = 3.3$ m

17. $b = 5.8$ yd, $h = 5.8$ yd

18. $b = 8.6$ in., $h = 0.8$ in.

_____

Practice 9-4

Areas of Parallelograms and Triangles

Find the area of each triangle.

1.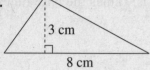

3 cm

8 cm

_____

2.

8 mm

6 mm

_____

3.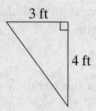

3 ft

4 ft

_____

Find the area of each parallelogram.

4.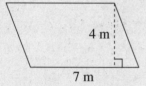

4 m

7 m

_____

5.

8 in.

5 in.

_____

6.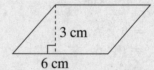

3 cm

6 cm

_____

Find the area of each complex figure.

7.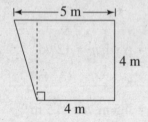

5 m

4 m

4 m

_____

8.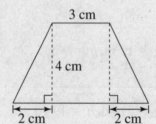

3 cm

4 cm

2 cm   2 cm

_____

9.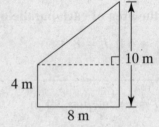

10 m

4 m

8 m

_____

10. Draw and label a triangle and a parallelogram that each have an area of 20 square units.

Tell whether each statement is *true* or *false*.

11. A parallelogram and triangle can have the same base and area. _____

12. Two triangles that have the same base always have the same area. _____

13. Any obtuse triangle has a greater area than any acute triangle. _____

Reteaching 9-5

Circles and Circumference

Parts of a Circle

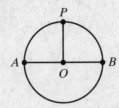

Point O is the center of the *circle*.
$\overline{AB}$ is a *diameter*.
$\overline{OA}$ is a *radius*. $\overline{OP}$ is also a radius.

In any circle, the length of the diameter is twice the length of the radius.

$$d = 2r$$

The radius is half the diameter.

$$r = \frac{d}{2}$$

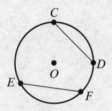

$\overline{CD}$ and $\overline{EF}$ are *chords*.
A diameter of a circle is the longest chord.

Circumference of a Circle

Circumference is the distance around a circle.

To find circumference:

- Multiply π times the diameter.

$$C = \pi d$$

- Or multiply π times twice the radius.

$$C = 2\pi r$$

To estimate the circumference of a circle, use 3 for π.

Estimate the circumference of a circle.

$$C \approx 3d$$
$$= 3 \times 8$$
$$= 24$$

The circumference is about 24 centimeters.

List each of the following for circle Q.

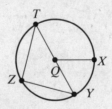

1. one diameter

_____

2. three chords

_____

3. three radii

_____

Find the unknown length for a circle with the given dimension.

4. $r = 8$ cm

$d = $ _____

5. $d = 110$ in.

$r = $ _____

6. $d = 48$ ft

$r = $ _____

Use 3 for π to estimate the circumference of a circle with the given radius or diameter.

7. $r = 12$ in. _____

8. $d = 15$ yd _____

9. $d = 7$ m _____

10. $d = 13$ ft _____

11. $r = 21$ yd _____

12. $r = 19$ cm _____

Practice 9-5

List each of the following for circle _O_.

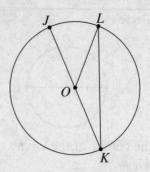

1. three radii   _____

2. one diameter   _____

3. two chords   _____

Find the unknown length for a circle with the given dimension.

4. $r = 4$ in.; $d = $?   5. $d = 15$ cm; $r = $?   6. $d = 9$ mm; $r = $?   7. $r = 12$ mm; $d = $?

_____   _____   _____   _____

Find the circumference of each circle. Round to the nearest unit.

8. 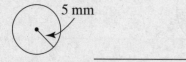   9.   10.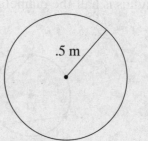

_____   _____   _____

11. 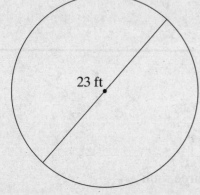   12.   13.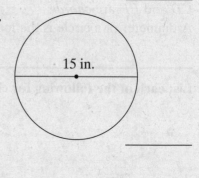

_____   _____   _____

Estimate the circumference of each circle with the given radius or diameter. Use 3 for π.

14. $d = 4$ in. _____ 15. $d = 8$ cm _____ 16. $r = 6$ m _____

17. $r = 10$ ft _____ 18. $r = 3$ in. _____ 19. $d = 20$ cm _____

Find the diameter of a circle with the given circumference. Round to the nearest unit.

20. $C = 128$ ft _____ 21. $C = 36$ cm _____ 22. $C = 200$ m _____

23. $C = 85$ in. _____ 24. $C = 57$ cm _____ 25. $C = 132$ in. _____

Reteaching 9-6

The formula for the *area of a circle* is:

Area = π × radius × radius

$A = \pi \times r \times r$

$A = \pi r^2$

Find the area of the circle.

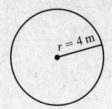

$A = \pi r^2$
$= \pi \times 4^2$
$= \pi \times 4 \times 4$
$= \pi \times 16$
$= 50.27$

The area is about 50.27 square meters.

Use $\frac{22}{7}$ for π when the radius or diameter of a circle is a multiple of 7 or a fraction.

Find the area of the circle.

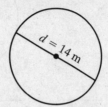

$d = 14$ m, so $r = 7$ m
$A = \pi r^2$
$= \frac{22}{7} \times 7^2$
$= \frac{22}{7} \times 7 \times 7$
$= \frac{22}{7} \times 7 \times 7$
$= 154$

The area is about 154 square meters.

Find the area of each circle. Round to the nearest tenth or use $\frac{22}{7}$ for π where appropriate.

1.
3 m

2.
2 m

3.
12 m

_____   _____   _____

4. $r = 8$ cm   **5.** $r = 13$ in.   **6.** $d = 28$ m   **7.** $d = 24$ ft

_____   _____   _____   _____

8. $r = 3\frac{1}{2}$ m   **9.** $d = 13$ cm   **10.** $r = 1\frac{3}{11}$ ft   **11.** $d = 29$ in.

_____   _____   _____   _____

Find the area of each circle to the nearest tenth. Use 3.14 for π.

12. $d = 23$ ft   **13.** $r = 2.5$ yd   **14.** $d = 48$ in.   **15.** $r = 19$ cm

_____   _____   _____   _____

Practice 9-6

Find the area of each circle. Round to the nearest tenth.

1.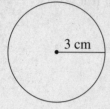

2.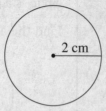

3.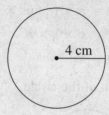

_____ _____ _____

Find the area of each circle. Round to the nearest unit. Use $\frac{22}{7}$ for π.

4.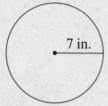

5.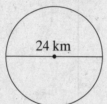

6.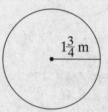

_____ _____ _____

Find the area of a circle with the given radius or diameter. Round to the nearest tenth.

7. $r = 12$ cm _____

8. $d = 15$ m _____

9. $d = 9$ cm _____

10. $d = 14$ cm _____

11. $r = 22$ m _____

12. $r = 28$ m _____

Solve each problem. Round to the nearest square inch.

13. Find the area of an 8-inch diameter pizza.

_____

14. Find the area of a 12-inch diameter pizza.

_____

15. The cost of the 8-inch pizza is $7.00. The cost of the 12-inch pizza is $12.50. Which size pizza is the better buy? Explain.

_____

_____

_____

Reteaching 9-7

Prisms and pyramids are three-dimensional figures. Their parts have special names.

- *Face*—flat surface on a prism or pyramid
- *Edge*—segment where two faces meet
- *Vertex*—point where edges meet

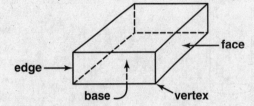

Prisms and pyramids can be named by the shape of their bases.

Prism

- has two *bases* congruent and parallel to one another

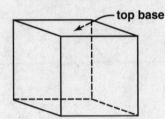

6 faces
12 edges
8 vertices

The bases are rectangles.
This prism is a *rectangular prism*.

Pyramid

- has one base; other faces are triangles

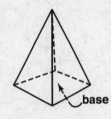

5 faces
8 edges
5 vertices

The base is a square.
This pyramid is a *square pyramid*.

Name each three-dimensional figure.

1.

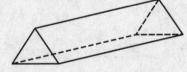

_____

2.

_____

3.

_____

4.

_____

5. How many faces, edges, and vertices does a pentagonal prism have?

_____

Practice 9-7

Name each three-dimensional figure.

1.

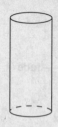

_____

2.

_____

3.

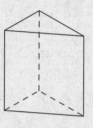

_____

4.

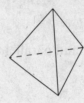

_____

5.

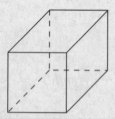

_____

6.

_____

7.

_____

8.

_____

9. In a square pyramid, what shape are the faces?

_____

10. How many faces does a rectangular prism have? How many edges? How many vertices?

_____

Reteaching 9-8

The *surface area* of a rectangular prism is the sum of the areas of the faces. You can use nets to find surface area.

Find the surface area of the prism.

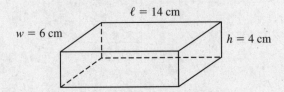

area of top = area of bottom
area of front = area of back
area of right side = area of left side

① Find the area of the top.
$A = \ell \times w$
$= 14 \times 6$
$= 84$ cm^2

② Find the area of the front.
$A = \ell \times h$
$= 14 \times 4$
$= 56$ cm^2

③ Find the area of the right side.
$A = w \times h$
$= 6 \times 4$
$= 24$ cm^2

④ Add.
$84 + 84 + 56 + 56 + 24 + 24 = 328$

The surface area of the prism is 328 square centimeters.

Find the surface area of each prism.

1.
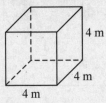

_____

2.
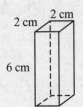

_____

3.
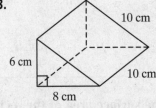

_____

Find the surface area of each cylinder. (*Hint:* The net of a cylinder is two circles and a rectangle.)

4.
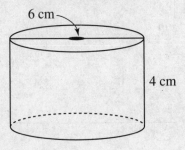

_____

5.
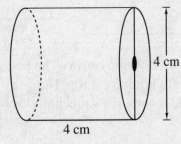

_____

Practice 9-8

Draw a net for each prism.

1.
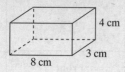

2.
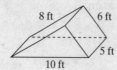

3.
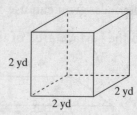

Find the surface area of each figure to the nearest whole unit.

4.
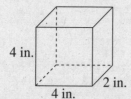

5.
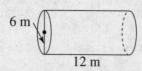

6.
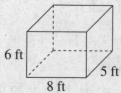

_____   _____   _____

7.
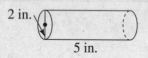

8.
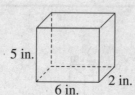

9.
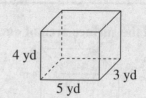

_____   _____   _____

Find the surface area of the rectangular prism with the given net.

10.
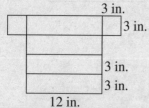

11.
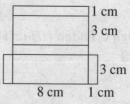

_____   _____

12. Jan is making a pencil holder out of plastic canvas. The pencil
holder will be 4 inches high. It will not have a top. The
circumference of the base is 9.42 inches. How much plastic
canvas does Jan need?   _____

13. Kerry is making a shadow box to display his models. It will be
8 in. high, 7 in. wide, and 5 in. deep. So he can see into the box,
it will not have a front. How much material will he need?   _____

Reteaching 9-9

Volumes of Rectangular Prisms and Cylinders

Volume is the number of cubic units needed to fill the space inside a three-dimensional figure. It is measured in cubic units.

Find the volume of the rectangular prism.

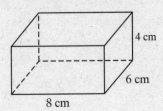

Volume = Area of base × height

$$V = B \times h$$
$$= \ell \times w \times h$$
$$= 8 \times 6 \times 4$$
$$= 192$$

The volume is 192 cubic centimeters.

Find the volume of the cylinder

$$V = B \times h$$

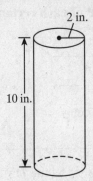

① Find the area of the base.

$$B = \pi \times r^2$$
$$= \pi \times 2^2$$
$$\approx 12.57$$

② Find the volume.

$$V = B \times h$$
$$= 12.57 \times 10$$
$$= 125.7$$

The volume is 125.7 cubic inches.

Find the volume of each rectangular prism.

1.

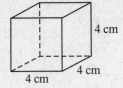

_____

2.

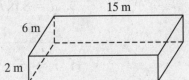

_____

3.

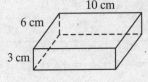

_____

Find the volume of each rectangular prism with the given dimensions.

4. $\ell = 6$ in., $w = 9$ in., $h = 3$ in.

_____

5. $\ell = 3.5$ cm, $w = 1.5$ cm, $h = 7$ cm

_____

6. $\ell = 16$ mm, $w = 18$ mm, $h = 2.5$ mm

_____

7. $\ell = 5$ m, $w = 6.2$ m, $h = 3.9$ m

_____

Find the volume of each cylinder. Round to the nearest tenth.

8. $r = 8$ m, $h = 9$ m

_____

9. $r = 12$ m, $h = 2$ m

_____

Practice 9-9

Volumes of Rectangular Prisms and Cylinders

Find the volume of each rectangular prism.

1.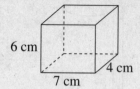

6 cm
4 cm
7 cm

_____

2.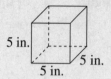

5 in.
5 in.
5 in.

_____

3.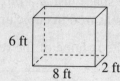

6 ft
8 ft
2 ft

_____

4. $\ell = 6$ cm, $w = 5$ cm, $h = 12$ cm

_____

5. $\ell = 13$ in., $w = 7$ in., $h = 9$ in.

_____

Find the volume of each cylinder. Round to the nearest whole unit.

6.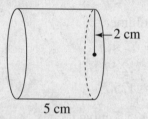

2 cm
5 cm

_____

7.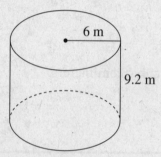

6 m
9.2 m

_____

8. $d = 14$ ft, $h = 28$ ft

_____

9. $d = 8$ ft, $h = 13$ ft

_____

10. $d = 14$ ft, $h = 14$ ft

_____

11. $r = 15$ ft, $h = 7$ ft

_____

12. A fish aquarium measures 3 feet long, 2 feet wide, and 2 feet high. What is the volume of the aquarium?

_____

13. A swimming pool is 25 feet wide, 60 feet long, and 7 feet deep. What is the volume of the pool?

_____

14. A cylindrical juice container is 9 in. tall and has a radius of 2 in. What is the volume of the container to the nearest whole unit?

_____

Reteaching 9-10

The store manager recorded 80 greeting cards sold on Friday. The day before she had sold one-half that number. On Wednesday, she sold 25 more than on Thursday. On Monday and Tuesday she sold a total of twice what she sold on Wednesday. How many cards did she sell during the 5 days?

Read and Understand

What does the problem ask you to find? *You need to find the total number of cards sold during the 5 days.*

Plan and Solve

How can you find the number sold on each day? *Use the information given in the problem. Work backward from that information to find the number sold on Thursday, then Wednesday, and finally, the total on Tuesday and Monday.*

Work backward.

Cards sold on Friday	80
80 ÷ 2 sold on Thursday	40
40 + 25 sold on Wednesday	65
2 × 65 sold on Monday and Tuesday	+ 130
	315

She sold 315 cards.

Look Back and Check

Write the number of cards sold as a mathematical expression. Solve by using the order of operations.

$$80 + (80 ÷ 2) + (40 + 25) + (2 × 65) = 315$$

Work backward to solve each problem.

1. On Friday, the diner served 56 ears of corn. On Thursday, the diner served one-half as much corn as on Friday. On Wednesday, the diner served two times as much as on Thursday. On Tuesday, the diner served one-half of what it had served on Wednesday. How much corn did the diner serve during the 4 days?

   _____

2. On Thursday, the diner served 42 pounds of green beans. On Wednesday, the diner served one-third that amount. On both Tuesday and Monday, the diner served one-half the amount it had served on Wednesday. How many pounds of beans did the diner serve during the 4 days?

   _____

3. On Friday, the diner served 60 baked potatoes. On both Tuesday and Thursday, the diner served one-fifth that amount. On both Monday and Wednesday, it served one-sixth of Thursday's amount. How many baked potatoes were served during the 5 days?

   _____

4. The diner served 32 pounds of salad on Saturday night. On both Friday and Thursday, one-half that amount was served. On Wednesday, one-eighth of Saturday's amount was served. How many pounds of salad did the diner serve during the 4 days?

   _____

Practice 9-10

Problem Solving: Work Backward

Work backward to solve each problem.

1. At the end of a board game, Al had 57 game dollars. During the game he had won $200, lost $150, won $25, lost $10, and lost $35. How much money did Al have at the start?

   _____

2. Jan spent half of the money she had on a coat. She spent half of what remained on a dress. Next, she spent half of what remained on a pair of boots. She returned home with $57. How much money did Jan have before shopping?

   _____

3. Bill gathered some eggs on Monday. On Tuesday, he gathered half as many eggs, plus an egg, as what he gathered on Monday. On Wednesday, he gathered half the difference of the number of eggs he gathered on Monday and Tuesday, plus an egg. If he gathered 5 eggs on Wednesday, how many eggs did Bill gather on Monday?

   _____

4. Carli spent a third of her money, and then spent $4 more. She then spent half of what money remained. It cost her $1 for the bus ride home. She then had $5 left. How much money did she start with?

   _____

5. Mick picked a number, doubled it, added 8, divided by 4, and had a result of 12. What number did Mick pick?

   _____

6. It takes Jenni 50 minutes to get ready for school. The drive to school takes 15 minutes. She needs 8 minutes to get to her locker, then to her first class. If school begins at 8:30 A.M., what is the latest Jenni should get up in the morning?

   _____

7. On May 31, Hayden's uncle and grandfather came to visit him. Hayden's grandfather visits every three days, and his uncle visits every twelve days. What is the first day in May that both visited Hayden on the same day?

   _____

Reteaching 10-1

Using a Number Line

The numbers . . . $-3, -2, -1, 0, +1, +2, +3,$ . . . are *integers*.
Integers are the set of positive whole numbers, their opposites, and 0.

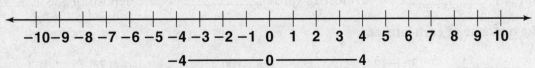

The absolute value of a number is its distance from 0 on a number
line. $|-4| = 4$. *Opposite integers*, like -4 and 4, are the same distance
from 0.

Compare -2 and 1.

For two integers on a number line, the greater integer is farther to the
right.

① Locate -2 and 1 on the number line.

② Find that 1 is farther to the right.

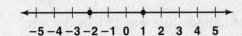

③ Write $1 > -2$ (1 is greater than -2),
or $-2 < 1$ (-2 is less than 1.)

Name the opposite of each integer.

1. 7 _____

2. -212 _____

3. 49 _____

4. 1,991 _____

5. -78 _____

6. 16 _____

Compare using < or >.

7. 6 ▢ 3

8. 2 ▢ 8

9. -2 ▢ 2

10. 9 ▢ -9

11. 0 ▢ 5

12. -9 ▢ -5

13. 0 ▢ 10

14. -5 ▢ -2

15. 7 ▢ -9

16. -5 ▢ -1

17. 6 ▢ -6

18. -12 ▢ 0

19. 8 ▢ -3

20. -1 ▢ -2

21. -5 ▢ 4

22. -3 ▢ -2

Find each absolute value.

23. $|-2|$

24. $|-100|$

25. $|-16|$

_____

_____

_____

26. $|8|$

27. $|-25|$

28. $|-250|$

_____

_____

_____

29. $|16|$

30. $|12|$

31. $|75|$

_____

_____

_____

Practice 10-1

Use an integer to represent each situation.

1. spent $23 _____

2. lost 12 yards _____

3. deposit of $58 _____

Name the opposite of each integer.

4. 16 _____

5. −12 _____

6. 100 _____

7. 75 _____

Find each absolute value.

8. $|-5|$ _____

9. $|13|$ _____

10. $|25|$ _____

11. $|-7|$ _____

Compare using < or >.

12. −5 ☐ 8

13. 13 ☐ −14

14. −11 ☐ −19

15. Order the temperatures from least to greatest. _____

   - The temperature was 25°F below zero.
   - The pool temperature was 78°F.
   - Water freezes at 32°F.
   - The low temperature in December is −3°F.
   - The temperature in the refrigerator was 34°F.

16. Graph these integers on the number line: −4, 9, 1, −2, 3.

Name the integer represented by each point on the number line.

17. *J* _____

18. *K* _____

19. *L* _____

20. *M* _____

Name an integer between the given integers.

21. −2, 9 _____

22. 3, −12 _____

23. −7, −11 _____

Complete with an integer that makes the statement true.

24. −9 > _____

25. _____ > 3

26. 0 > _____

Think of the days of a week as integers. Let today be 0, and let days in the past be negative and days in the future be positive.

27. If today is Tuesday, what integer stands for last Sunday? _____

28. If today is Wednesday, what integer stands for next Saturday? _____

29. If today is Friday, what integer stands for last Saturday? _____

30. If today is Monday, what integer stands for next Monday? _____

Reteaching 10-2

Adding Integers

You can add integers on a number line.

Example 1: Find $4 + 3$.

Start at 0. Move 4 units right and then 3 units right.

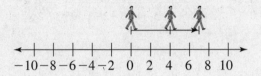

$4 + 3 = 7$

Example 2: Find $-3 + -2$.

Start at 0. Move 3 units left and then 2 units left.

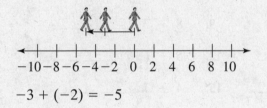

$-3 + (-2) = -5$

Example 3: Find $5 + (-3)$.

Start at 0. Move 5 units right and then 3 units left.

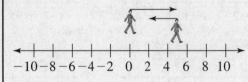

$5 + (-3) = 2$

Example 4: Find $-4 + 1$.

Start at 0. Move 4 units left and then 1 unit right.

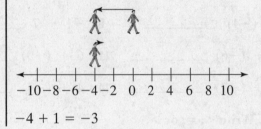

$-4 + 1 = -3$

Use the number line to find each sum.

1. $3 + 2$ _____

2. $6 + 4$ _____

3. $-4 + (-1)$ _____

4. $-4 + (-8)$ _____

5. $4 + (-1)$ _____

6. $-6 + 8$ _____

7. $-7 + 3$ _____

8. $-5 + 8$ _____

9. $3 + 5$ _____

10. $-3 + (-5)$ _____

11. $3 + (-5)$ _____

12. $-3 + 5$ _____

Find each sum.

13. $-6 + (-4)$ _____

14. $7 + (-2)$ _____

15. $-1 + (-6)$ _____

16. $9 + (-2)$ _____

17. $-6 + (-6)$ _____

18. $13 + 3$ _____

19. $-14 + (-5)$ _____

20. $5 + (-12)$ _____

21. $-9 + 9$ _____

22. $18 + (-18)$ _____

23. $0 + (-4)$ _____

24. $6 + 0$ _____

25. $15 + (-15)$ _____

26. $-12 + 0$ _____

27. $-9 + 10$ _____

28. $12 + (-11)$ _____

29. $-12 + 11$ _____

30. $2 + (-10)$ _____

Practice 10-2

Write a numerical expression for each model. Find each sum.

1. _____

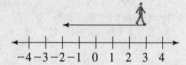

2. _____

3. _____

Use a number line or mental math to find each sum.

4. $-2 + (-8)$ _____

5. $8 + (-4)$ _____

6. $-6 + 3$ _____

7. $6 + (-4)$ _____

8. $-1 + 7$ _____

9. $-8 + 3$ _____

10. $-2 + (-6)$ _____

11. $6 + (-9)$ _____

12. $-5 + (-7)$ _____

13. $-4 + (-7)$ _____

14. $4 + (-7)$ _____

15. $-4 + 7$ _____

Compare. Write <, =, or >.

16. $-5 + (-6)$ ☐ $6 + (-5)$

17. $-8 + 10$ ☐ $-3 + 6$

18. $-4 + (-9)$ ☐ $-8 + (-5)$

19. $20 + (-12)$ ☐ $-12 + (-4)$

Solve.

20. Bill has overdrawn his account by $15. There is a $10 service charge for an overdrawn account. If he deposits $60, what is his new balance?

_____

21. Jody deposited $65 into her savings account. The next day, she withdrew $24. How much of her deposit remains in the account?

_____

22. The outside temperature at noon was 9°F. The temperature dropped 15 degrees during the afternoon. What was the new temperature?

_____

23. The temperature was 10° below zero and dropped 24 degrees. What is the new temperature?

_____

24. The high school football team lost 4 yards on one play and gained 9 yards on the next play. What is the total change in yards?

_____

25. Philip earned $5 for shoveling snow and received $8 allowance. He spent $6 at the movies. How much money does he have left?

_____

Reteaching 10-3

To subtract an integer, add the opposite.

Example 1: Subtract $5 - 8$.

Add the opposite: $5 + (-8)$

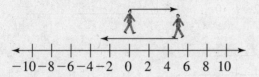

$5 - 8 = -3$

Example 2: Subtract $2 - (-4)$.

Add the opposite: $2 + 4$

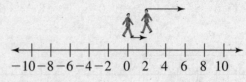

$2 - (-4) = 6$

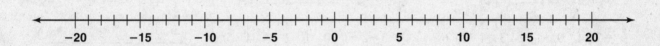

Use a number line. Find each difference.

1. $3 - (-6)$ _____

2. $2 - (-4)$ _____

3. $-1 - 2$ _____

4. $-3 - (-5)$ _____

5. $-8 - (-3)$ _____

6. $4 - (-4)$ _____

7. $-8 - 2$ _____

8. $8 - (-2)$ _____

9. $-8 - (-2)$ _____

10. $-7 - 4$ _____

11. $-10 - 2$ _____

12. $-5 - (-5)$ _____

13. $-5 - 6$ _____

14. $9 - (-3)$ _____

15. $-11 - (-6)$ _____

Find each difference.

16. $15 - (-4)$ _____

17. $-12 - 3$ _____

18. $21 - (-7)$ _____

19. $3 - (-12)$ _____

20. $-2 - 10$ _____

21. $-13 - 13$ _____

22. $5 - (-5)$ _____

23. $18 - (-10)$ _____

24. $-7 - (-13)$ _____

25. $14 - 16$ _____

26. $3 - 15$ _____

27. $-6 - (-9)$ _____

28. $-12 - 6$ _____

29. $15 - (-9)$ _____

30. $7 - 19$ _____

Solve each equation.

31. $12 + s = -10$ _____

32. $x - 8 = -3$ _____

33. $b + 18 = 12$ _____

34. $x - 21 = -2$ _____

35. $s - 25 = -100$ _____

36. $y + 5 = 9$ _____

37. $-5 + c = -10$ _____

38. $x + 30 = 5$ _____

39. $15 + b = 10$ _____

Practice 10-3

Write a numerical expression for each model. Find each difference.

1.

_____

2.

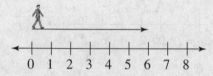

_____

3.

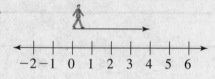

_____

4.

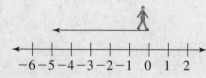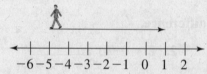

_____

Find each difference.

5. $2 - 5$ _____ **6.** $-5 - 2$ _____ **7.** $-6 - 3$ _____

8. $10 - (-3)$ _____ **9.** $-9 - (-2)$ _____ **10.** $0 - (-5)$ _____

11. $-12 - (-3)$ _____ **12.** $8 - 13$ _____ **13.** $11 - (-6)$ _____

Compare using <, =, or >.

14. $5 - 12$ ☐ $5 - (-12)$ **15.** $8 - (-5)$ ☐ $-8 - 5$

16. $9 - (-4)$ ☐ $4 - (-9)$ **17.** $-12 - 12$ ☐ $12 - (-12)$

Solve each equation.

18. $t + 15 = 10$ _____ **19.** $8 + c = 3$ _____ **20.** $x - 12 = -3$ _____ **21.** $s + 6 = 1$ _____

Solve.

22. The temperature was 48°F and dropped 15° in two hours. What was the temperature after the change? _____

23. The temperature at midnight is −5°C and is expected to drop 12° by sunrise. What is the expected temperature at sunrise? _____

24. Catherine has $400 in her checking account. She writes a check for $600. What is the balance in her account? _____

25. On the first play, the football team lost 6 yards. On the second play, the team lost 5 yards. What was their total change in yards? _____

Reteaching 10-4

When two integers have like signs, the product will always be positive.

Both integers are positive: $3 \times 4 = 12$

Both integers are negative: $-3 \times (-4) = 12$

When two integers have different signs, the product will always be negative.

One integer positive, one negative: $3 \times (-4) = -12$

One integer negative, one positive: $-3 \times 4 = -12$

Example 1: Find -8×3.

① Determine the product.
$8 \times 3 = 24$

② Determine the sign of the product. Since one integer is negative and one is positive, the product is negative.

③ So, $-8 \times 3 = -24$.

Example 2: Find $(-10) \times (-20)$.

① Determine the product.
$10 \times 20 = 200$

② Determine the sign of the product. Since both integers are negative, the product is positive.

③ So, $(-10) \times (-20) = 200$.

Find each product.

1. $7 \times (-4)$

2. $-5 \times (-9)$

3. -11×2

4. $8 \times (-9)$

5. $15 \times (-3)$

6. $-7 \times (-6)$

7. -12×6

8. $13 \times (-5)$

9. $-10 \times (-2)$

10. A dog lost 2 pounds three weeks in a row. What integer expresses the total change in the dog's weight? _____

Find each quotient.

11. $18 \times (-6)$

12. $-35 \times (-7)$

13. -15×3

14. $28 \times (-4)$

15. $25 \times (-5)$

16. $-27 \times (-9)$

17. -12×4

18. $33 \times (-11)$

19. $-50 \times (-2)$

Practice 10-4

peak**Multiplying Integers**

Use a number line to find each product.

1. 5×2 **2.** -4×3 **3.** $6 \times (-2)$ **4.** $-3 \times (-2)$

_____   _____   _____   _____

Find each product.

5. 7×8 **6.** -5×7 **7.** $4 \times (-8)$ **8.** $-8 \times (-2)$

_____   _____   _____   _____

9. $11 \times (-6)$ **10.** -7×6 **11.** $-8 \times (-8)$ **12.** 10×4

_____   _____   _____   _____

13. 21×13 **14.** -15×12 **15.** $-25 \times (-14)$ **16.** $10 \times (-25)$

_____   _____   _____   _____

Find the missing number.

17. $3 \times \underline{\ ?\ } = -6$ **18.** $4 \times \underline{\ ?\ } = -4$ **19.** $\underline{\ ?\ } \times (-4) = -8$

_____   _____   _____

20. $-3 \times \underline{\ ?\ } = 9$ **21.** $-9 \times (-2) = \underline{\ ?\ }$ **22.** $\underline{\ ?\ } \times (-2) = -18$

_____   _____   _____

23. Your teacher purchases 24 pastries for a class celebration, at
$2 each. What integer expresses the amount he paid?

_____

24. Temperatures have been falling steadily at 5°F each day. What
integer expresses the change in temperature in degrees 7 days
from today?

_____

25. A submarine starts at the surface of the Pacific Ocean and
descends 60 feet every hour. What integer expresses the
submarine's depth in feet after 6 hours?

_____

26. A skydiver falls at approximately 10 meters per second. Write a
number sentence to express how many meters he will fall in
40 seconds.

_____

Reteaching 10-5

When two integers have like signs, the quotient will always be positive.

Both integers are positive:	$8 \div 2 = 4$
Both integers are negative:	$-8 \div (-2) = 4$

When two integers have different signs, the quotient will always be negative.

One integer positive, one negative:	$8 \div (-2) = -4$
One integer negative, one positive:	$-8 \div 4 = -2$

Example 1: Find $-24 \div 8$.

① Determine the quotient.
$24 \div 8 = 3$

② Determine the sign of the quotient. Since one integer is negative and one is positive, the quotient is negative.

③ So, $-24 \div 8 = -3$.

Example 2: Find $35 \div (-7)$.

① Determine the quotient.
$35 \div 7 = 5$

② Determine the sign of the quotient. Since one integer is positive and one is negative, the quotient is negative.

③ So, $35 \div (-7) = -5$.

Find each quotient.

1. $18 \div (-6)$

_____

2. $-35 \div (-7)$

_____

3. $-15 \div 3$

_____

4. $28 \div (-4)$

_____

5. $25 \div (-5)$

_____

6. $-27 \div (-9)$

_____

7. $-12 \div 4$

_____

8. $33 \div (-11)$

_____

9. $-50 \div (-25)$

_____

Solve each equation.

10. $-2y = 12$

_____

11. $\frac{p}{10} = -6$

_____

12. $-10y = -100$

_____

13. $7x = -28$

_____

14. $-6x = 36$

_____

15. $\frac{s}{-2} = -14$

_____

16. $\frac{x}{8} = -12$

_____

17. $4x = -24$

_____

18. $3x = 30$

_____

19. A ship sank at a rate of 90 feet in 10 seconds.
Represent the rate of change with an integer. _____

Practice 10-5

Find each quotient.

1. $14 \div 7$

2. $21 \div (-3)$

3. $-15 \div 5$

4. $-27 \div (-9)$

_____

_____

_____

_____

5. $45 \div (-9)$

6. $-42 \div 6$

7. $-105 \div (-15)$

8. $63 \div (-9)$

_____

_____

_____

_____

9. $108 \div 6$

10. $-204 \div 17$

11. $240 \div (-15)$

12. $-252 \div (-12)$

_____

_____

_____

_____

Solve each equation.

13. $-6x = -24$

14. $\frac{t}{4} = -32$

15. $5m = 45$

_____

_____

_____

16. $3b = -27$

17. $\frac{c}{2} = -17$

18. $\frac{a}{4} = 4$

_____

_____

_____

19. $-15 = 3z$

20. $-2x = 100$

21. $-22 = \frac{m}{11}$

_____

_____

_____

Represent each rule of change with an integer.

22. spends $300 in 5 days

23. runs 800 feet in 4 minutes

_____

_____

24. descends 45 yards in 15 sec

25. lose 26 ounces of baby fat in 13 months

_____

_____

26. Juan's baseball card collection was worth $800. Over the last 5 years, the collection decreased $300 in value. What integer represents the average decrease in value each year?

_____

27. Florence purchased stock for $20 per share. After 6 days, the stock is worth $32 per share. What integer represents the average increase in stock value each day?

_____

28. A freight train starts out at 0 miles per hour. After 15 miles the train is traveling 90 miles per hour. What integer represents the average increase in speed per mile?

_____

Reteaching 10-6

Graphing in the Coordinate Plane

Example: Graph (2, −4).

- 2 is the *x-coordinate*. It tells how far to move left or right from the origin.

- −4 is the *y-coordinate*. It tells how far to move up or down from the origin.

Find the coordinates of point *A*.

① Start at the origin.

② How far left or right? *3 left*
   The *x-coordinate* is −3.

③ How far up or down? *5 up*
   The *y-coordinate* is 5.

The coordinates of point *A* are (−3, 5).

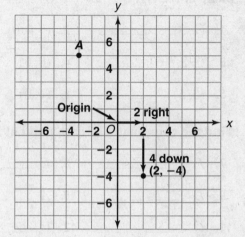

Graph each point in a coordinate plane.

1. *B* (1, 6) **2.** *C* (−4, −3)

3. *D* (0, 5) **4.** *E* (−2, 2)

5. *F* (−1, −5) **6.** *G* (6, −4)

7. *H* (5, 5) **8.** *J* (4, 0)

9. *K* (−4, −4) **10.** *L* (2, −3)

11. *M* (−2, 0) **12.** *N* (5, −1)

13. *P* (0, −3) **14.** *Q* (−4, 0)

Find the coordinates of each point.

15. *R* ————— **16.** *S* —————

17. *T* ————— **18.** *U* —————

Look at the coordinate grid above.

19. If you travel 7 units down from *S*, at which point will you be located?

   ——————

20. If you travel 4 units right from *T* and 2 units down, at which point will you be located?

   ——————

Practice 10-6

Graphing in the Coordinate Plane

Name the point with the given coordinates in the coordinate plane at the right.

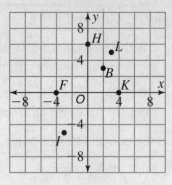

1. $(2, 3)$ _____   2. $(-4, 0)$ _____

3. $(-3, -5)$ _____   4. $(0, 6)$ _____

5. $(3, 5)$ _____   6. $(4, 0)$ _____

Find the coordinates of each point at the right.

7. J _____   8. E _____

9. D _____   10. A _____

11. G _____   12. C _____

Graph each point on a coordinate plane.

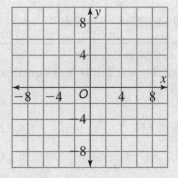

13. $A(8, -4)$ 14. $B(-4, 8)$

15. $C(4, 8)$ 16. $D(-8, -4)$

17. $E(8, 4)$ 18. $F(-4, -8)$

19. A taxi begins at $(4, -3)$. It travels 3 blocks west and 5 blocks north to pick up a customer. What are the customer's coordinates?

_____

20. A moving truck fills up a shipment at an old address, at $(-2, 1)$. It travels 7 blocks south and 6 blocks east to the new address. What is the location of the new address?

_____

Use the coordinate plane below.

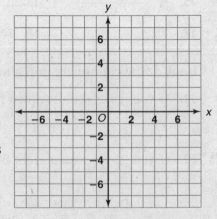

21. Graph four points on the coordinate plane so that when the points are connected in order, the shape is a rectangle. List the coordinates of the points.

_____

22. Graph four points on the coordinate plane so that when the points are connected in order, the shape is a parallelogram that is not a rectangle. List the coordinates of the points.

_____

Reteaching 10-7

To find a *balance,* add the income (positive number) and the expenses (negative number). The sum is the balance.

Balance Sheet for Lunch Express		
Month	**Income**	**Expenses**
January	$1,095	−$459
February	$1,468	−$695
March	$1,773	−$700
April	$602	−$655

- To find the balance for February, add

  $1,468 + (−695) = 773.$

  Lunch Express made a profit of $773.

- To find the balance for April, add

  $602 + (−655) = −53.$

  Lunch Express had a loss of $53.

To look for a trend in the data, draw a line graph of the monthly balances.

- Balances range from −$53 to $1,073. Make the vertical scale from −$200 to $1,100. Use intervals of $100.

- Use the horizontal scale for the months.

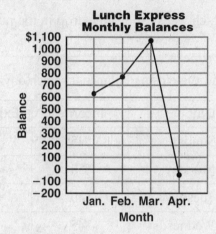

The trend was for increasing balances— until April.

Find each sum or difference.

1. −$9 + $17

2. $51 − $83

3. $42 − (−$18)

4. −$77 + $92

5. −$109 + $109

6. $28 − $4310

7. −$156 + $429

8. $232 − (−$97)

9. −$401 − $582

10. $1,874 − (−$1,892)

11. $6,012 + (−$3,933)

12. −$4,401 − (−$1,560)

13. A company earned $2,357 in January. The company earned $2,427 in February and $1,957 in March. The company's total expenses for the first quarter were $4,594. What was the company's profit?

14. Your bank account is overdrawn $31. The bank charges $20 for being overdrawn. You deposit $100. What is the balance of your bank account?

Practice 10-7

Use the graph at the right for Exercises 1–4.

1. How many basketballs were sold in the third week? _____

2. How many basketballs were sold in the fifth week? _____

3. How many more basketballs were sold in the fourth week than were sold in the third week? _____

4. Which weeks showed a drop in the number of basketballs sold?

_____

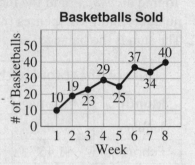

Basketballs Sold

5. Find the closing balance for each day.

Day	Income	Expenses	Balance
Sunday	$45	−$32	
Monday	$50	−$40	
Tuesday	$40	−$26	
Wednesday	$45	−$50	
Thursday	$30	−$35	
Friday	$60	−$70	
Saturday	$60	−$53	

6. Draw a line graph to show the balances in Exercise 5.

7. On which day did the greatest balance occur?

_____

8. On which day did the least balance occur?

_____

9. On which two days was the balance the same?

_____

10. What was the total balance for the week? Was it a loss or profit?

_____

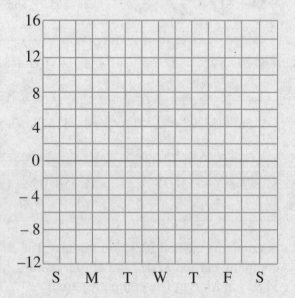

Reteaching 10-8

A table or a graph can show how the input and output of a *function* are related.

Make a table to show how number of feet is a function of number of yards.

Input (yards)	Output (feet)
1	3
2	6
3	9
4	12
5	15

The table shows that for every yard, there are 3 feet. You multiply the number of yards by 3 to find the number of feet.

Use the values in the table to draw a graph of the function.

① Locate the points from the table: $(1, 3), (2, 6), (3, 9), (4, 12), (5, 15)$

② Draw a line through the points.

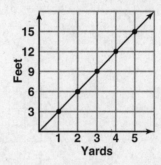

Complete the table.

1.

Input	Output
1	4
2	5
3	6
4	
5	

2.

Input	Output
4	2
6	4
8	6
10	
12	

3.

Input	Output
2	10
3	15
4	20
5	
6	

Complete each table given the rule. Then graph the function.

4. cups as a function of quarts

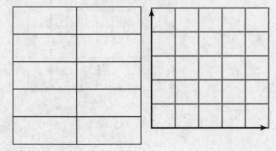

5. days as a function of weeks

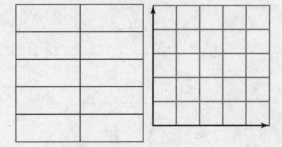

Practice 10-8

Complete the function table given the rule.

1. Rule: Output = Input · 5

Input	1	2	3	4	5
Output	5	10	15		

2. Rule: Output = Input · 2

Input	10	20	30	40	50
Output	20	40	60		

3. Rule: Output = Input + 3

Input	3	4	5	6	7
Output	6	7	8		

Make a table and graph each function. Use *x*-values of −2, −1, 0, 1, and 2.

4. $y = x - 1$

5. $y = 3x$

6. $y = \frac{x}{2} - 1$

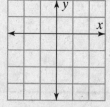
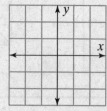
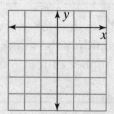

Graph each function.

7.

Hours	Wages ($)
1	15
2	30
3	45
4	60

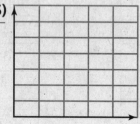

8.

Gallons	Quarts
1	4
2	8
3	12
4	16

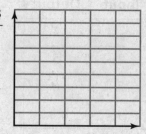

9. A parking garage charges $3.50 per hour to park. The function rule = 3.5 h shows how the number of hours h, relates to the parking charge c. Graph the function.

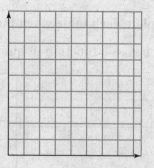

Reteaching 10-9

Stuart is from Australia, where speed limits are measured in kilometers per hour. While visiting the United States, Stuart drives along a road with a speed limit of 50 miles per hour (mph). Stuart would like to know the equivalent speed in kilometers per hour (kph). He remembers that 15 mph = 25 kph, and 30 mph = 50 kph.

Read and Understand	15 mph = 25 kph, and 30 mph = 50 kph. You need to approximate 50 miles per hour in kilometers per hour.
Plan and Solve	You can approximate 50 miles per hour in kilometers per hour by *making a line graph*. Stuart knows two pairs of equivalent speeds. Plot the points (15, 25) and (30, 50) on a coordinate plane and connect them with a line.
Look Back and Check	"50 miles per hour is about 83 kilometers per hour" can be written as (50, 83). You can see that this point is on the line drawn.

Solve each problem by making a graph.

1. The federal minimum wage in 1965 was $1.25 per hour. In 1980, the minimum wage was $3.10 per hour. In 2000, it was $5.50 per hour. Estimate the minimum wage in 1990.

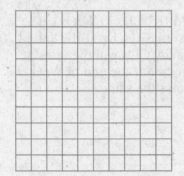

2. In 1989, there were 960,000 civilians working for the military. In 1993, this number decreased to 850,000. How many civilians were working for the military in 1991?

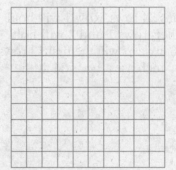

Practice 10-9

Solve each problem by making a graph.

1. If 4 apples equals $1 and 2 apples $.50, how much do 15 apples cost? There are no quantity discounts.

2. If you saved $2 on January 1, $4 on February 1, $6 on March 1, $8 on April 1, and so on, how much money would you save in one year?

3. In 1995 the price of a soccer ball was $8.00. A financial analyst predicted that the price would increase $.25 per year for the next 10 years. In what year will the price be $9.75?

4. One gallon of gas costs $1.50. Three gallons of gas costs $4.50. How much will 9 gallons of gas cost?

5. A parking lot has 24 rows. Row 1 will hold 100 cars. Together, rows 1 and 2 will hold 200 cars. How many cars will the first 12 rows hold if each row increases the total at the same rate?

6. A company sold 185 CDs in Week 1. The company then sold 370 CDs at the end of Week 2. How many CDs will the sales department forecast at the end of Week 9 if the sales rate stays the same?

Reteaching 11-1

Probability

The *probability of an event* is a number that describes how likely it is that the event will occur. When the outcomes are equally likely, the probability of an event is the following ratio.

$$P(\text{event}) = \frac{\text{number of favorable outcomes}}{\text{total number of outcomes}}$$

Find the probability of choosing the red chip if the chips are placed in a bag and mixed.

$$P(\text{red}) = \frac{\text{number of favorable outcomes}}{\text{total number of outcomes}} = \frac{1}{5}$$

The probability of choosing the red chip is $\frac{1}{5}$.

- If an event is impossible, its probability is 0. The probability of drawing an 11 from cards numbered 1 to 10 is impossible.

- If an event is unlikely, equally likely, or likely, its probability is between 0 and 1. The probability that you will draw a 2 or a 4 from cards numbered 1 to 10 is likely.

- If an event is certain, its probability is 1. The probability that you will draw a card from 1 to 10 from a set of cards numbered 1 to 10 is certain.

Find the probability of each event.

1. You pick a vowel from the letters in EVENT. _____

2. You pick a weekend day from days of the week. _____

3. You pick a month that begins with the letter J. _____

4. A spinner is labeled 1–6. You spin 1 or 5. _____

5. You pick an odd number from 75 to 100. _____

6. You pick a word with four letters from this sentence. _____

7. You have a birthday on February 30. _____

8. A number cube is tossed. You toss a 1, 3, or 5. _____

Each of the 26 letters in the English alphabet is put on a slip of paper. One slip is selected at random. Classify each event as *impossible, unlikely, likely*, or *certain*.

9. $P(\text{consonant})$

10. $P(\text{a letter from A to Z})$

11. $P(\text{vowel})$

_____

_____

_____

12. $P(\text{B})$

13. $P(10)$

14. $P(*)$

_____

_____

_____

Practice 11-1

A number cube is rolled once. Find each probability. Write your answer as a fraction, a decimal, and a percent.

1. $P(3)$ _____

2. $P(\text{even})$ _____

3. $P(1, 3, \text{or } 5)$ _____

4. $P(0)$ _____

5. $P(1 \text{ or } 6)$ _____

6. $P(1 \text{ through } 6)$ _____

A spinner is divided into 5 equal sections. You spin the spinner once.

7. Find the probability that the spinner lands on a white section.

    _____

8. Find the probability that the spinner lands on a dark section.

    _____

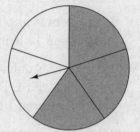

Use the words _impossible, unlikely, even chance, likely,_ and _certain_ to help you describe each event. Then find the probability.

9. Rolling a blue on a cube painted with 3 blue faces and 3 yellow faces.

    _____

10. Drawing a nickel from a bag containing 7 dimes and 3 nickels.

    _____

11. Spinning a yellow if a spinner with 12 equal regions has 10 yellow regions.

    _____

12. Choosing a name that starts with H from a phone book page that begins with Hardy and ends with Hoffman.

    _____

A stack of cards is placed face down. Each card has one letter of the word EXCELLENT. Find each probability. Write as fraction, decimal, and percent.

13. $P(E)$

    _____

14. $P(N)$

    _____

15. $P(T \text{ or } X)$

    _____

16. $P(\text{consonant})$

    _____

Reteaching 11-2

A *fair* game generates equally likely outcomes. To decide whether a game is fair:

① Make a list of all the possible outcomes of the game.

② Determine whether each player has about the same probability of winning.

The Spinner Game

Spin a spinner with equal-size sections numbered 1–8. Player A wins on a multiple of 2 or 3. Player B wins on any other number. Is this game fair?

① Possible outcomes: 1, 2, 3, 4, 5, 6, 7, 8.

② Player A wins with a 2, 3, 4, 6, and 8. Player B wins with a 1, 5, 7.

P(A winning) = $\frac{5}{8}$, P(B winning) = $\frac{3}{8}$

The game is not fair.

You can use the results of playing a game to find the *experimental probability* of each player winning.

Example: Two players played a game 25 times. Player A won 15 times and player B won 10 times.

$P(\text{A wins}) = \frac{\text{number of times A won}}{\text{total games played}}$

$= \frac{15}{25}$

$= \frac{3}{5}$

$P(\text{B wins}) = \frac{\text{number of times B won}}{\text{total games played}}$

$= \frac{10}{25}$

$= \frac{2}{5}$

You and your friend play a game. You win if you roll a number cube and it lands on 5. Your friend wins if she rolls a number cube and it lands on a factor of 6.

1. What is the probability that you win? _____

2. What is the probability that your friend wins? _____

3. Is the game fair? Explain your reasoning.

_____

The line plot shows the results of rolling a number cube 20 times. Find the experimental probability.

4. $P(6)$ _____

5. $P(\text{less than 4})$ _____

6. $P(\text{greater than 3})$ _____

7. $P(\text{even number})$ _____

8. $P(\text{prime number})$ _____

```
                              X
              X           X   X
        X  X      X       X
        X  X  X  X  X  X
        X  X  X  X  X  X
     ←──────────────────────→
        1  2  3  4  5  6
```

Practice 11-2

Mirga and José played a game and completed the table.

Mirga wins	ЖЖ ЖЖ ЖЖ ЖЖ ЖЖ I
José wins	ЖЖ I
Times played	ЖЖ ЖЖ ЖЖ ЖЖ ЖЖ ЖЖ II

1. Find the experimental probability that Mirga wins.

_____

2. Find the experimental probability that José wins.

_____

3. Do you think the game is fair? Explain.

_____

The table below shows the results of spinning a spinner 15 times. Find each experimental probability.

Trial	1	2	3	4	5	6	7	8
Outcome	blue	yellow	red	blue	green	red	yellow	blue

Trial	9	10	11	12	13	14	15
Outcome	blue	green	red	blue	blue	green	red

4. P(red) _____   5. P(yellow) _____   6. P(green) _____   7. P(blue) _____

One day, 40 members who came to an athletic club were asked to complete a survey. Use the results below to find each probability.

Question	Result
Are you male or female?	28 male, 12 female
Are you under 26 years old?	24 yes, 16 no

8. P(male) _____   9. P(26 or older) _____

For Exercises 10–11, refer to the table, which shows the results of tossing a number cube 20 times. Is each game fair? Explain.

Outcome	1	2	3	4	5	6
Number of Times Rolled	1	2	4	6	2	5

10. Player A wins if the number is even. Player B wins if the number is odd.

_____

11. Player A wins if the number is 2. Player B wins if the number is 5.

_____

Reteaching 11-3

Making Predictions From Data

Sometimes you cannot survey an entire *population*. Instead, you survey a *sample*—a part of the population that can be used to make predictions about the entire population.

A city has 5,000 sixth graders. To estimate the number of sixth graders who ride bicycles to school, a random sample was used. Of the 200 sixth graders chosen, 40 said they ride bicycles to school. Predict the number of sixth graders out of 5,000 who ride bicycles to school.

① Write a proportion. $\frac{40}{200} = \frac{n}{5,000}$

② Solve. $200 \times n = 40 \times 5,000$

$$200n = 200,000$$

$$n = \frac{200,000}{200}$$

$$n = 1,000$$

The sample suggests that 1,000 sixth graders ride bikes to school.

Identify the sample size. Then make a prediction for the population.

1. How many in a class of 100 students prefer banana yogurt to other flavors? Of 10 students asked, 6 prefer banana.

   Sample size _____

   Prediction for population _____

2. How many of the 1,900 joggers seen at the park like to run at 6 A.M.? Of 190 joggers asked, 35 like to run at 6 A.M.

   Sample size _____

   Prediction for population _____

3. Of 600 first graders in the school district, 109 are not yet reading. How many first graders out of 180,000 in the entire state are not yet reading?

   Sample size _____

   Prediction for population _____

4. Out of 300 families, 150 read the morning newspaper. There are 2,400 families in town. How many read the morning newspaper?

   Sample size _____

   Prediction for population _____

5. How many in a town of 500 students walk to school? Of 100 students asked, 32 walked to school.

   Sample size _____

   Prediction for population _____

6. Out of 150 families, 16 drive sport utility vehicles (SUVs). How many of the 4,500 families in the county drive SUVs?

   Sample size _____

   Prediction for population _____

Practice 11-3

Answer each question in a complete sentence and in your own words.

1. What is a population?

   _____

   _____

2. What is a sample?

   _____

   _____

3. How can you predict the number of times an event will occur?

   _____

   _____

   _____

The probability of an event is 20%. How many times should you expect the event to occur in the given number of trials?

4. 15 trials   5. 40 trials   6. 75 trials   7. 120 trials

   _____   _____   _____   _____

Write and solve a proportion to make each prediction.

8. In a sample of 400 customers at a fast food restaurant, it was determined that 156 customers ordered a salad. The restaurant typically has 1,200 customers in a day. Predict how many of these customers will order a salad.

   _____

9. Before a company delivers 600 strings of lights, it tests a sample. A quality inspector examines 75 strings of lights and finds that 3 are defective. Predict how many strings of lights in the delivery are defective.

   _____

10. A company manufactures egg timers. An inspector finds that there are 22 defective timers in a sample of 500. Predict how many egg timers are defective in a shipment of 4,250 egg timers.

    _____

Reteaching 11-4

Problem Solving: Simulate a Problem

You have six different-color pairs of loose socks in a drawer. You reach into the drawer without looking and take out two socks. What is the probability you will pick a matched pair?

Read and Understand

How many socks are in the drawer? 12

How many different colors are there? 6

What are the possible results of picking two socks?
You can pick two socks of the same color or two socks of different colors.

What are you trying to find? *The probability of picking two socks of the same color.*

Plan and Solve

You can simulate the problem by making a spinner like the one at the right. Each number stands for one of the six colors. Spin the spinner twice to find the colors of the two socks. Record whether the colors are the same or different.

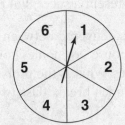

Repeat the simulation many times. Divide the number of times the colors were the same by the total number of simulations to find the experimental probability of getting a matched pair.

Look Back and Check

What other methods could you use to simulate the problem?
Randomly pick two cards from six matched pairs of cards.

Simulate and solve each problem. Show all your work.

1. You have four pairs of different-color loose socks in a drawer. You pick 2 socks without looking. What is the probability that you will get a matched pair? Use a spinner with 8 equal sections. Let each section represent one sock.

2. You have 5 different-color pens and 2 different-color pencils in your pocket. You pick a pen and a pencil without looking. What is the probability that you will pick the red pen and red pencil? Use real pens and pencils to simulate this event.

3. Each day a restaurant offers a special sandwich made with one of three different meats and one of three different cheeses. Your favorite is salami with American cheese. What is the probability that your favorite is the special of the day? Use two spinners, each with three equal sections: one spinner for the meats and one for the cheeses.

4. In the refrigerator, you have 3 different juices in bottles and 4 different sodas in cans. Your favorites are the orange juice and the ginger ale. If you pick a juice and a soda without looking, what is the probability that you will get both your favorites? Use one spinner with three sections and one with four. Let the first spinner represent the bottles and the second, the cans.

Practice 11-4

Simulate and solve each problem. Show all your work.

1. Marty makes 60% of his free throws.

   a. What is the probability that he will make two free throws in a row? Use a spinner with 5 equal sections. Let 3 sections represent a successful free throw.

   b. Marty practices and can now make 80% of his free throws. What is the probability that he will make two free throws in a row? Use the same spinner from part (a), but let 4 sections represent a successful free throw.

2. Mail is delivered between 12:00 P.M. and 1:00 P.M. every day to Joe's house. Joe comes home for lunch at 11:30 A.M. for 45 minutes. What is the probability that the mail will arrive during Joe's lunch break? Use two spinners like those shown below.

Choose a strategy to solve each problem. Show all your work.

3. You have several coins that total 38 cents. You have the same number of pennies as nickels. How many coins do you have?

4. There were 10 people at a party. At the end of the party, each person shook hands with each of the others. How many hand shakes were there in all?

5. Use two number cubes to find the experimental probability that both teams will win today's games. Let 1, 2, and 3 on one cube represent a softball win and let 1, 2, 3, 4, and 5 on the other cube represent a football win.

Chances of Winning Games	
Sport	**Probability**
Softball	$\frac{1}{2}$
Football	$\frac{5}{6}$

Reteaching 11-5 ....

Your choices for your new car are an exterior color of white, blue, or black, and an interior of fabric or leather.

A *tree diagram* shows all possible choices. Each branch shows one choice.

color	interior	outcome
white	fabric	white fabric
	leather	white leather
blue	fabric	blue fabric
	leather	blue leather
black	fabric	black fabric
	leather	black leather

The tree diagram shows 6 choices. Choosing your car at random, the probability of picking a white car with leather interior is

$$P(\text{white, leather}) = \frac{1}{6}.$$

You can use the *counting principle* to find the total number of choices.

> When there are m ways of making one choice and n ways of making a second choice, then there are $m \times n$ ways to make the first choice followed by the second choice.

Exterior choices		Interior choices		Total
3	$\times$	2	$=$	6

There are 6 possible choices for your car.

Draw a tree diagram to find each probability. Show your work.

1. Marva can have a small, medium, or large salad. She can have Italian, French, or Russian dressing on it. Find the probability that she choses a small salad with French dressing.

   _____

2. You flip a coin two times. Find the probability of getting tails on both tosses.

   _____

Use the counting principle to find the total number of outcomes.

3. There are 4 kinds of fruit, 2 kinds of cereal, and 2 kinds of milk. How many ways can a bowl of cereal, fruit, and milk be chosen?

   _____

4. There are 4 choices for skis, 2 choices for bindings, and 5 choices for boots. How many ways can skis, bindings, and boots be chosen?

   _____

5. There are 3 pairs of jeans, 2 vests, and 5 shirts. How many ways can jeans, a vest, and a shirt be chosen?

   _____

6. There are 10 yogurt flavors, 4 syrups, and 5 toppings. How many ways can one flavor, one syrup, and one topping be chosen?

   _____

Practice 11-5

Tree Diagrams and the Counting Principle

Each shape in a set of blocks comes in two sizes (small and large), three colors (yellow, red, and blue), and two thicknesses (thick and thin).

1. Draw a tree diagram to find the total number of outcomes.

2. How many outcomes are possible?

   _____

3. How many outcomes will be red?

   _____

4. How many outcomes will be blue and thin?

   _____

5. How many outcomes will be large?

   _____

6. Show how you could use the counting principle to find the number of outcomes.

   _____

7. Suppose a medium size is also available. How many outcomes are possible now?

   _____

Use the counting principle to find the total number of outcomes.

8. You toss a coin 8 times.

   _____

9. A restaurant offers 12 types of entrees, 6 types of appetizers, and 4 types of rice. How many meals of appetizer, entree, and ice are there?

   _____

Find each probability using the counting principle.

10. spinning a 3 each time you spin the spinner 3 times

    _____

11. spinning a 9 if you spin the spinner 20 times

    _____

12. getting two odd numbers in a row if you roll a number cube twice

    _____

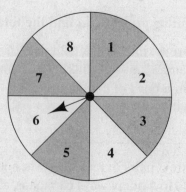

Reteaching 11-6 ....

An arrangement of items in a particular order is a *permutation*.

Find the number of permutations for lining up Leah, Brian, and Ahmad for a photograph. You can use these different methods.

- Draw a tree diagram.

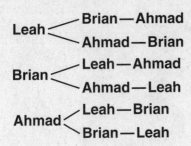

- Make an organized list.
    Leah, Brian, and Ahmad
    Leah, Ahmad, and Brian
    Brian, Leah, and Ahmad
    Brian, Ahmad, and Leah
    Ahmad, Leah, and Brian
    Ahmad, Brian, and Leah

- Use the counting principle.

    In how many ways can the first person be chosen? *3 ways*

    In how many ways can the middle person be chosen? *2 ways*

    In how many ways can the remaining person be chosen? *1 way*

    $$3 \times 2 \times 1 = 6$$

There are 6 permutations of Leah, Brian, and Ahmad.

Make an organized list or a tree diagram to find the permutations of each set of numbers or letters. Use each item exactly once.

1. the letters COW

_____

2. the numbers 2, 3, and 8

_____

3. the letters IF

_____

4. the numbers 7 and 9

_____

Use a tree diagram, a list, or the counting principle to find the number of permutations of each set.

5. A basketball team has 5 starting players. In how many ways can their names be announced before the game?

_____

6. In how many ways can 8 songs on a CD be played if you use the shuffle feature on your CD player?

_____

7. Three students are waiting for the cafeteria to open. In how many ways can they enter the food line?

_____

8. For how many consecutive baseball games can the manager use a different batting order for 9 players?

_____

Practice 11-6

1. Make an organized list of how Ali, Ben, and Chou can sit in a row.

2. Make an organized list to find the permutations of the letters in the word BITE. How many of the permutations are English words?

   _____

3. Draw a tree diagram to find the two-number permutations of the numbers 2, 4, 6, and 8. Use each number exactly once.

4. Mrs. Schoup has three errands to do on her way home from work.

   a. Draw a tree diagram to find the permutations of going to the post office, the library, and the gas station.

   b. How many different ways can Mrs. Schoup organize her errands?

   _____

5. Vince has homework in math, science, language, and reading. How many different ways can he do his homework?

   _____

6. The spring program will feature songs from five grade levels. How many different ways can these grade levels be arranged?

   _____

7. How many different ways can six posters be displayed side-by-side?

   _____

8. How many different ways can you scramble the letters in the word CAT?

   _____

Reteaching 11-7

Events are *independent* when the occurrence of one event does not affect the other event. If two events are independent, the probability that both will occur is the product of their probabilities.

Example 1: A ball is drawn from the bag, its color noted, and then put back into the bag. Then another ball is drawn. Are the two events independent?

The events are independent because the color of the first ball drawn does not affect the color of the next ball drawn.

A *compound event* consists of two or more separate events.

Example 2: Find the probability that a red ball is drawn, replaced, and then a blue ball is drawn at random.

- Probability of drawing a red ball is $\frac{2}{5}$.
- Probability of drawing a blue ball is $\frac{1}{5}$.

$$P(\text{red}) \times P(\text{blue})$$
$$= \frac{2}{5} \times \frac{1}{5}$$
$$= \frac{2}{25}$$

The probability of drawing a red ball, replacing it, and then drawing a blue ball at random is $\frac{2}{25}$.

Decide whether or not the events are independent. Write *yes* or *no*.

1. You pick a green ball from the bag above. You keep the ball out, and pick a red ball. _____

2. You toss five coins. _____

3. You get three 4's on three rolls of a number cube. _____

4. You select a colored marker from a package of colored markers. Your teacher selects one after you. _____

Find the probability for each situation.

5. A letter is chosen from the words BABY GIRL and then replaced.

   Find $P(\text{Y and R})$.

   _____

6. A letter is chosen from the words BABY BOY and then replaced.

   Find $P(\text{B and B})$.

   _____

A number cube is rolled and a coin is tossed. Find the probability of each event.

7. the number 6 and tails _____

8. an even number and heads _____

9. a number less than 1 and heads _____

10. an odd number and tails _____

11. A coin is tossed three times. Find the probability that the coin lands on tails, then heads, then tails. _____

Practice 11-7 •••

Decide whether or not the events are independent. Explain your answers.

1. You draw a red marble out of a bag. Then you draw a green marble.

_____

2. You draw a red marble out of a bag and put it back. Then you draw a green marble.

_____

3. You roll a number cube 3 times.

_____

The spinner at the right is spun twice. Find the probability…

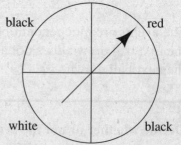

4. both red   **5.** white, then black   **6.** both black

_____   _____   _____

7. white, then red   **8.** both white   **9.** black, then red

_____   _____   _____

10. Are the spins independent events? Explain

_____

A number cube is rolled three times. Find the probability of each sequence of rolls.

11. 2, 3, 6   **12.** odd, even, odd   **13.** all greater than 1

_____   _____   _____

Suppose each letter of your name is printed on a separate card.

14. One card is drawn from a container holding first-name letters. Find *P*(first letter of your first name).

_____

15. One card is drawn from a container holding last-name letters. Find *P*(first letter of your last name).

_____

16. One card is drawn from each container. Find *P*(your initials).

_____

•••••••• **Lesson 11-7 Practice** •••••••••••••••••••••••••• *Course 1* Chapter 11

Name _____ Class _____ Date _____

Reteaching 12-1

Solving Two-Step Equations

Some equations contain two operations. To solve them, use inverse operations to get the variable alone on one side of the equation. Begin by undoing addition or subtraction. Then undo multiplication or division.

Example: Solve $2d + 1 = 9$.

$$2d + 1 = 9$$

$2d + 1 - \mathbf{1} = 9 - \mathbf{1}$ Subtract 1 from each side to undo the addition.

$\dfrac{2d}{\mathbf{2}} = \dfrac{8}{\mathbf{2}}$ Divide each side by 2 to undo the multiplication.

$d = 4$ Simplify.

$2 \cdot 4 + 1 \overset{?}{=} 9$ Check your work by substituting 4 for d in the equation and solving.

$9 = 9$ Since $9 = 9$, the solution is correct.

---

1. Solve $7x - 5 = 16$.

   a. What must you first do to both sides? _____

   b. What must you next do to both sides? _____

   c. What is the solution? _____

2. Solve $12 = \frac{t}{5} + 8$.

   a. What must you first do to both sides? _____

   b. What must you next do to both sides? _____

   c. What is the solution? _____

Solve each equation. Check the solution.

3. $7y - 6 = 8$

   _____

4. $81 = 3x - 6$

   _____

5. $\frac{c}{8} + 10 = 15$

   _____

6. $2f - 6 = 4$

   _____

7. $4k + 20 = 24$

   _____

8. $\frac{e}{5} + 100 = 120$

   _____

Practice 12-1

Solving Two-Step Equations

Explain what was done to the first equation to get the second equation.

1. $\frac{x}{5} - 3 = 12 \; : \; x = 75$

_____

_____

2. $6x + 7 = 31 \; : \; x = 4$

_____

_____

3. $\frac{x}{3} + 2 = 4 \; : \; x = 6$

_____

_____

Solve each equation. Check the solution.

4. $3x + 7 = 37$

$x =$ _____

5. $31 = 7x - 11$

$x =$ _____

6. $11k - 84 = 92$

$k =$ _____

7. $4r + 13 = 57$

$r =$ _____

8. $\frac{z}{4} + 16 = 21$

$z =$ _____

9. $7 = \frac{t}{6} - 3$

$t =$ _____

10. $6q - 18 = 30$

$q =$ _____

11. $\frac{w}{15} + 26 = 42$

$w =$ _____

12. $15u + 18 = 18$

$u =$ _____

13. $9 = 7b - 12$

$b =$ _____

14. $\frac{x}{11} + 21 = 35$

$x =$ _____

15. $\frac{s}{7} - 11 = 17$

$s =$ _____

16. Hideki baked 41 cookies. He gave the same number of cookies to each of 5 friends, saving 11 cookies for himself. How many cookies did each friend receive?

_____

17. Estelle is buying dresses by mail. She pays $65 for each dress, plus a shipping and handling charge of $8 for the entire order. If her order costs $268, how many dresses did she buy?

_____

18. Ms. Juarez planted a 7-foot-tall tree. The height (h) of the tree, in feet, after n years is given by the equation $h = 4n + 7$. In how many years will the height be 39 feet?

_____

Reteaching 12-2

An *inequality* contains $<, >, \leq, \geq,$ or $\neq$. Unlike the equations you have worked with, an inequality may have many solutions.

The *solutions of an inequality* are the values that make the inequality true. They can be graphed on a number line. An open circle shows that the number below it is not a solution. A closed circle shows that the number below it is a solution.

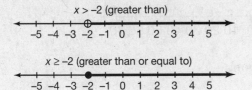

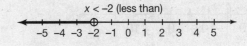

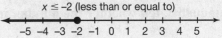

Example: Graph the inequality $x > 4$.

The inequality is read as "x is greater than 4." Since all numbers to the right of 4 are greater than 4, you can draw an arrow from 4 to the right. Since 4 is not greater than itself, use an open circle on 4.

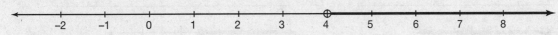

---

1. Graph the inequality $x \leq -4$.

   a. Write the inequality in words. _____

   b. Will the circle at -4 be open or closed? _____

   c. Graph the solution.

        $-7 \quad -6 \quad -5 \quad -4 \quad -3 \quad -2 \quad -1 \quad 0 \quad 1 \quad 2 \quad 3$

2. Graph the inequality $x \geq -1$.

   a. Write the inequality in words. _____

   b. Will the circle at -1 be open or closed? _____

   c. Graph the solution.

        $-5 \quad -4 \quad -3 \quad -2 \quad -1 \quad 0 \quad 1 \quad 2 \quad 3 \quad 4 \quad 5$

3. Graph the inequality $x < 4$.

   a. Write the inequality in words. _____

   b. Will the circle at 4 be open or closed? _____

   c. Graph the solution.

        $-4 \quad -3 \quad -2 \quad -1 \quad 0 \quad 1 \quad 2 \quad 3 \quad 4 \quad 5 \quad 6$

Practice 12-2

Graph each inequality on a number line.

1. $x \le 3$

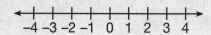

2. $t > 1$

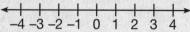

3. $q \ge -10$

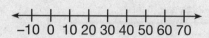

4. $m < 50$

For each inequality, tell whether the number in bold is a solution.

5. $x < 7;$ **7** _____

6. $p > -3;$ **3** _____

7. $k \ge 5;$ **0** _____

8. $3z \le 12;$ **4** _____

9. $n - 5 > 3;$ **6** _____

10. $2g + 8 \ge 3;$ **−1** _____

Write an inequality for each graph.

11. _____

12. _____

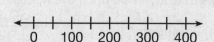

Write a real-world statement for each inequality.

13. $d \ge 60$

_____

14. $p < 200$

_____

Write and graph an inequality for each statement.

15. You can walk there in 20 minutes or less.

_____

16. Each prize is worth over $150.

_____

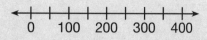

17. A species of catfish, *malapterurus electricus*, can generate up to 350 volts of electricity.

a. Write an inequality to represent the amount of electricity generated by the catfish.

_____

b. Draw a graph of the inequality you wrote in part (a).

Reteaching 12-3

You can solve an inequality by using inverse operations to get the variable alone.

Example 1: Solve $x - 7 \leq 2$. Then check the solution.

$$x - 7 \leq 2$$
$$x - 7 + 7 \leq 2 + 7 \quad \text{Add 7 to both sides.}$$
$$x \leq 9$$

Check. Test a number greater than 9 and another number less than 9.

Try 11. $11 - 7 \leq 2$ Try 5. $5 - 7 \leq 2$
 $4 \leq 2$ false $-2 \leq 2$ true

Example 2: Solve $a + 15 > 10$. Then check the solution.

$$a + 15 > 10$$
$$a + 15 - 15 > 10 - 15 \quad \text{Subtract 15 from both sides.}$$
$$a > -5$$

Test a number greater than -5 and another number less than -5.

Try 0. $0 + 15 > 10$ Try -6. $-6 + 15 > 10$
 $15 > 10$ true $9 > 10$ false

Solve each inequality.

1. $x + 8 < 15$

_____

2. $y + 2 > 8$

_____

3. $a - 5 \geq -1$

_____

4. $x - 10 \leq -11$

_____

5. $y - 7 \geq 2$

_____

6. $d - 18 \geq 2$

_____

7. $13 + c \leq 33$

_____

8. $-12 + b \geq 4$

_____

9. $4 + w \geq 18$

_____

10. $x + 15 < -9$

_____

Practice 12-3

Solve each inequality.

1. $x - 5 < 15$　　**2.** $m + 7 \geq 12$　　**3.** $k + 5 < -10$　　**4.** $15 + w \geq 4$

_____　_____　_____　_____

5. $g - (-4) \geq 0$　**6.** $-6 > b - 24$　　**7.** $f - 6 < 12$　　**8.** $d + 8 \geq 2$

_____　_____　_____　_____

9. $q + 9 < 60$　　**10.** $h + (-1) > -1$　**11.** $42 + p \geq 7$　　**12.** $-27 > a - 5$

_____　_____　_____　_____

Write an inequality for each sentence. Then solve the inequality.

13. Five is greater than a number minus 2. _____

14. Twenty is less than or equal to a number plus 4. _____

15. A number minus 5 is greater than 25. _____

16. A number plus 18 is less than or equal to 20. _____

Write an inequality for each problem. Then solve the inequality.

17. You and the chess teacher have been playing chess for 18 minutes. To make the chess club, you must win the game in less than 45 minutes. How much time do you have to win the chess game?

_____

18. Your phone card allows you to talk long distance for up to 120 minutes. You have been on a long distance call for 72 minutes. How much longer do you have to talk before your phone card expires?

_____

Solve each inequality mentally.

19. $9x < 108$　　　　　**20.** $s - 18 \geq 12$　　　　**21.** $t + 5 < -15$

_____　　　_____　　　_____

22. $\frac{1}{6}g > 20$　　　　**23.** $k \div 4 \geq 25$　　　　**24.** $24 > b + 16$

_____　　　_____　　　_____

Name _____ Class _____ Date _____

Reteaching 12-4

Problem Solving: Comparing Strategies

You can sometimes draw a diagram or write an equation to solve a problem.

Example Kristin staked out a rectangular garden that has one side measuring 6 ft. If the area of the garden is 48 ft, what are the dimensions of the garden?

Read and Understand

The area of a rectangular garden is 48 ft^2. One side is 6 ft long.

Plan and Solve

Method 1: Draw a diagram.

Draw a row of 6 equal squares to represent one side of the garden.

Add rows to the diagram until you have 48 total squares.

The rectangle is 6 squares long and 8 squares wide, so the garden is 6 ft × 8 ft.

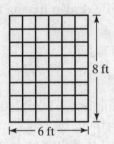

Method 2: Write and solve an equation.

Use the formula for the area of a rectangle.

$l \cdot w = A$

$6 \cdot w = 48$

$w = 8$

The garden is 6 ft × 8 ft.

Look Back and Check

The length times the width of the garden must equal the area of the garden.

$6 \cdot 8 \stackrel{?}{=} 48$

$48 = 48$ The answer checks.

Choose a strategy and solve each problem.

1. Carlos is packing mugs in a box with a bottom that is 56 centimeters by 72 centimeters. In order to prevent the mugs from breaking, Carlos needs a square with area 64 centimeters^2 for each mug. Assuming he doesn't stack the mugs, how many mugs can he fit in the box?

   _____

3. Beth uses one-foot wide square tiles to cover a rectangular area. The rectangle has 16 tiles on one side, and she uses 192 tiles to cover the area. What are the dimensions of the rectangle?

   _____

2. Agatha is hiking along a 150-mile trail. She hikes 10% of the trail the first day and 15% of the trail the second day. How many miles of the trail are left?

   _____

4. Todd is stacking boxes against a wall that is 12 m high. If he has stacked 3 boxes and the pile reaches halfway to the ceiling, what is the height of each box?

   _____

Practice 12-4

Solve each problem by either drawing a diagram or writing an equation. Explain why you chose the method you did.

1. Derrick is thinking of a negative integer. When he multiplies the integer by itself and then adds three times the integer to the product, he gets 180. What is Derrick's integer?

   _____

2. During a pancake making contest, Team A made 8 more pancakes than Team B. Team C made twice as many pancakes as Team B. Together, the three teams made a total of 72 pancakes. How many pancakes did Team A make?

   _____

3. The area of a rectangle is 18 square inches. How many rectangles whose sides are measured in whole numbers can be drawn having this area?

   _____

Choose a strategy to solve each problem.

4. Howard plans to drive from Seattle, Washington, to Portland, Oregon, a road distance of 172 miles. He needs to be in Portland by 11:45 A.M. If he drives at a rate of 60 miles per hour, what is the latest time he can leave Seattle?

   _____

5. Heather and Denise are running laps. They start together at the same starting point. Heather completes a lap every 120 seconds, and Denise completes a lap every 96 seconds. In how many seconds will they again meet at the starting point?

   _____

6. A triangle has angles D, E, and F. The complement of $\angle D$ is 42°, and the supplement of $\angle E$ is 54°. What is the measure of $\angle F$?

   _____

7. Ernesto, Michelina, and Kale volunteer at the zoo. Ernesto works every 5 days. Michelina works every 6 days. Kale works every 15 days. They work together today. How many days will it be until the next time they work together?

   _____

8. Cassie is lining up 45 students in the chorus. She wants each row to have the same number of students. She also wants the number of students in each row to be a prime number. What are her options?

   _____

Reteaching 12-5

A *perfect square* is the square of a whole number. The number 81 is a perfect square because it is the square of 9.

You can also say that 9 is the *square root* of 81, or $\sqrt{81} = 9$. The square root of a given number is a number that, when multiplied by itself, is the given number. You can use a calculator to find square roots.

Example 1

a. Find $\sqrt{4}$.

Since $2 \times 2 = 4$, $\sqrt{4} = 2$.

b. Find $\sqrt{75}$.

$\sqrt{75} \approx 8.6602540$

You can estimate square roots using perfect squares.

Example 2

Tell which two consecutive whole numbers $\sqrt{52}$ is between.

$49 < 52 < 64$	Find perfect squares close to 52.
$\sqrt{49} < \sqrt{52} < \sqrt{64}$	Write the square roots in order.
$7 < \sqrt{52} < 8$	Simplify.

$\sqrt{52}$ is between 7 and 8.

Determine if each number is a perfect square.

1. 24 _____ **2.** 36 _____ **3.** 49 _____ **4.** 121 _____

Find each square root.

5. $\sqrt{9}$ _____ **6.** $\sqrt{25}$ _____ **7.** $\sqrt{4}$ _____

8. $\sqrt{100}$ _____ **9.** $\sqrt{400}$ _____ **10.** $\sqrt{2,500}$ _____

Use a calculator to tell whether each number is a perfect square.

11. 576 _____ **12.** 1,200 _____ **13.** 2,401 _____

14. 900 _____ **15.** 1,521 _____ **16.** 1,875 _____

Tell which two consecutive whole numbers the square root is between.
Use a calculator to find each square root to the nearest tenth.

17. $\sqrt{42}$ _____ **18.** $\sqrt{88}$ _____ **19.** $\sqrt{63}$ _____

20. $\sqrt{75}$ _____ **21.** $\sqrt{30}$ _____ **22.** $\sqrt{97}$ _____

Practice 12-5

Exploring Square Roots and Rational Numbers

Determine if each number is a perfect square.

1. 90 _____ **2.** 225 _____ **3.** 49 _____ **4.** 28 _____

5. 289 _____ **6.** 144 _____ **7.** 240 _____ **8.** 1000 _____

Find each square root.

9. $\sqrt{196}$ _____ **10.** $\sqrt{4}$ _____ **11.** $\sqrt{289}$ _____ **12.** $\sqrt{16}$ _____

13. $\sqrt{361}$ _____ **14.** $\sqrt{64}$ _____ **15.** $\sqrt{1}$ _____ **16.** $\sqrt{25}$ _____

17. $\sqrt{9}$ _____ **18.** $\sqrt{484}$ _____ **19.** $\sqrt{256}$ _____ **20.** $\sqrt{400}$ _____

Use a calculator to find each square root to the nearest hundredth.

21. $\sqrt{10}$ _____ **22.** $\sqrt{48}$ _____ **23.** $\sqrt{28}$ _____ **24.** $\sqrt{55}$ _____

25. $\sqrt{72}$ _____ **26.** $\sqrt{37}$ _____ **27.** $\sqrt{86}$ _____ **28.** $\sqrt{98}$ _____

29. $\sqrt{946}$ _____ **30.** $\sqrt{14}$ _____ **31.** $\sqrt{62}$ _____ **32.** $\sqrt{316}$ _____

Tell which consecutive whole numbers each square root is between.

33. $\sqrt{8}$ **34.** $\sqrt{3}$ **35.** $\sqrt{40}$ **36.** $\sqrt{14}$

_____ _____ _____ _____

37. $\sqrt{75}$ **38.** $\sqrt{120}$ **39.** $\sqrt{54}$ **40.** $\sqrt{129}$

_____ _____ _____ _____

Tell whether each number is rational.

41. $\frac{2}{9}$ _____ **42.** $\sqrt{16}$ _____ **43.** $\sqrt{32}$ _____ **44.** $7.\overline{4}$ _____

45. $\sqrt{48}$ _____ **46.** $\frac{12}{5}$ _____ **47.** $8.\overline{65}$ _____ **48.** $\sqrt{24}$ _____

49. The largest pyramid in Egypt, built almost 5,000 years ago, covers an area of about 63,300 square yards. Find the length of each side of the square base.

_____

50. Square floor tiles frequently have an area of 929 square centimeters. Find the length of a side of one of these tiles.

_____

Reteaching 12-6

Introducing the Pythagorean Theorem

The *hypotenuse* of a right triangle is the side opposite the right angle and is the longest side. The other two sides are called *legs*. In the shown triangle, sides a and b are the legs. Side c is the hypotenuse.

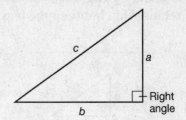

The *Pythagorean Theorem* states that the sum of the squares of the lengths of the legs of a right triangle is equal to the square of the length of the hypotenuse. This can be written algebraically as $a^2 + b^2 = c^2$.

Example

Find the missing length.

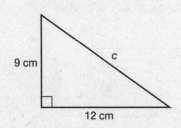

$a^2 + b^2 = c^2$	Use the Pythagorean Theorem to find the length of side c.
$9^2 + 12^2 = c^2$	Substitute 9 for a and 12 for b.
$81 + 144 = c^2$	Square 9 and 12.
$225 = c^2$	Add.
$15 = c$	Find $\sqrt{225}$.

The length of the hypotenuse is 15 cm.

Find the missing side length of each right triangle.

1.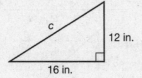

_____

2.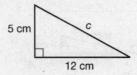

_____

3.

_____

4.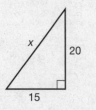

_____

5.

_____

6.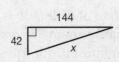

_____

7.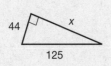

_____

8.

_____

9.

_____

10. An 8-foot ladder is leaning against a building. If the bottom of the ladder is 3 feet from the base of the building, how far is it up the building from the bottom of the ladder to the top of the ladder? Round to the nearest tenth of a foot. _____

Practice 12-6

Use the Pythagorean Theorem to write an equation expressing the relationship between the legs and the hypotenuse for each triangle.

1. _____

2. _____

3. _____

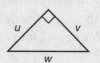

Find the missing side length of each right triangle.

4. $a = 10, b = 24, c = ?$

5. $a = ?, b = 35, c = 37$

6. $a = 39, b = ?, c = 89$

_____   _____   _____

Find the missing side length of each right triangle.

7. $t = $ _____

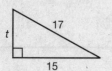

8. $d = $ _____

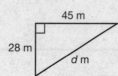

9. $m = $ _____

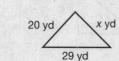

10. $x = $ _____

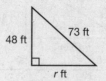

11. $u = $ _____

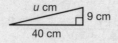

12. $r = $ _____

13. The state of Colorado is shaped like a rectangle, with a base measuring about 385 miles and a height of about 275 miles. About how far is it from the northwest corner to the southeast corner of Colorado?

_____

14. A drawing tool is shaped like a right triangle. One leg measures about 14.48 centimeters, and the hypotenuse measures 20.48 centimeters. What is the length of the other leg? Round your answer to the nearest hundredth of a centimeter.

_____

15. An 8-foot ladder is leaned against a wall from 4 feet away. How high up the wall does the ladder reach? Round your answer to the nearest tenth of a foot.

_____